BABEL

My three decades with
the Defense Language Institute

WE SPEAK YOUR LANGUAGE

日本語 中国话 한국어
РУССКИЙ العربية ESPAÑOL
DEUTSCH زبان فارسى TÜRKÇE
PORTUGUÊS ČESKY HRVATSKI
СРПСКИ FRANÇAIS ITALIANO
BAHASA INDONESIA POLSKI
ROMÂNĂ SHQIP MAGYAR
NEDERLANDS ENGLISH
Tiếng Việt اُردو हिन्दी KURDÎ
TAGALOG پښتو دری Ўзбек
ภาษาไทย ΕΛΛΗΝΙΚΑ עברית

Benjamín De La Selva

Copyright © 2015 by
Benjamín De La Selva

All rights reserved under International and Pan-American Copyright Convention. No parts of this book may be reproduced or retransmitted in any form or by any means without written permission from the author.

Published with consent of the Defense Language Institute, Foreign Language Center, Monterey, California

For more information contact:

Benjamín De La Selva
P.O. Box 5788, Monterey, CA 93944

Cover:
The Tower of Babel by Pieter Bruegel the Elder (1563).
The aforementioned painting has been identified on the internet as being free of known restrictions under copyright law, including all related and neighboring rights.

Published in the United States of America

ISBN: 978-1519691316

INTRODUCTION

The Tower of Babel refers to the biblical tower built in an attempt to reach heaven. As a punishment, God created many different languages so that the workers could not understand one another.

The Babel of ancient times and our present Babel share only one thing in common: "Both are famous for languages." However, while the former was disrupted by the creation of multiple languages, the latter flourishes by the teaching of them.

This book is a compilation of articles I wrote for the DLI Globe and the quarterly newsletters of the DLI Alumni Association, during the years 1992 and 2005. It is divided into six sections: General, Evolution, Berlin Wall Monument, Memorial Day and War Accounts, Language Programs, and Personalities.

General History includes broad information about DLI's history, faculty composition, and languages taught.

My DLI and Vietnam Experience recounts my own experiences as student, teacher, supervisor, staff, and dean of every DLI school up to 2004.

Evolution encompasses DLI's progress in many areas such as Team Teaching, course development, technology in the DLI classroom, and others.

The Berlin Wall Monument narrates major events leading to the arrival of this monument on the DLI campus.

Memorial Day and War Accounts contains stories about individual alumni who participated in U.S. conflicts and others who died in those conflicts.

Language Programs includes aspects and description of several language programs: Arabic, German, Russian, Spanish, and Serbian-Croatian.

Personalities consists of short articles about faculty and other individuals who were remembered at the time of their passing.

Hall of Fame presents DLI hall of fame inductees in 2006, 2007, and 2011.

DLIAA and DLIF merger introduces the joining of the DLI Alumni Association and the DLI Foundation.

I hope you enjoy reading this book. *Ben De La Selva*

Note 1: The articles about the Russian (p.111) and German (p.118) programs were written by Dr. Luba Grant, and Ms. Annette Scheibner, respectively, and are published with their permission.

Note 2: DLI and DLIFLC will be used interchangeably throughout this book. Likewise Serbo-Croatian, Serbian-Croatian, and Serbian/Croatian (see p.100).

ACKNOWLEDGMENTS

This book is dedicated to all the faculty, staff, and students of the Defense Language Institute in Monterey, California, with special thanks to the faculty of the Asian, European and Latin American, Korean, Middle East, Persian, Russian, and Slavic Schools during the years 1972 to 2005. Likewise, I owe gratitude to the following DLI commandants and friends for supporting me throughout my DLI career and beyond:

Col. John Hook (Jul72-Sep74); Col. James Koenig, (Sep74-Aug75)
Col. Samuel Stapleton (Aug75-Sep78); Col. Thomas G. Foster III (Sep78-Jun81)
Col. David McNerney (Jun81-Aug85); Col. Monte R. Bullard (Aug85-Oct87)
Col. Todd Poch (Oct87-Sep88); Col. Ronald Cowger (AF) (Sep88-Aug89)
Col. Donald Fischer (Aug89-Jan93); Col. Vladimir Sobichevsky (Jan93-Dec95)
Col. Ila Mettee Mc-Cutchon (Dec95-Feb96); Col. Daniel Devlin (Feb96-Dec00)
Col. Kevin Rice (Dec00-Jun03); Col. Michael R. Simone (Jun03-Aug05)
Col. Tucker Mansager (Aug05-Oct07); Col. Sue Ann Sandusky (Oct07-May10)
Col. Danial D. Pick (May10-Apr14); Col. David K. Chapman (Apr14-Jun15)
Col. Phillip J. Deppert (Jun2015-Present)

Dr. Ray T. Clifford, Provost and Chancellor
Dr. Stephen Payne, Provost and DLIFLC Historian
Dr. Betty Lou Leaver, Provost
Mr. Steven Collins, DLIFLC Chief of Staff
Mr. Cameron Binkley, DLIFLC Deputy Historian
Dr. Jorge Kattan, Chair, Spanish department
Mr. DJ Skelton, President, DLI Foundation
Dr. Howard Rowland, Arabic and Russian professor
Ms. Natela Cutter, DLIFLC Public Affairs Chief
Dr. Christine Campbell, Associate Provost, Continuing Education

Mr. Shawn Cardella, DLIAA Co-Founder
Mr. Arthur Douglas, DLIAA Co-Founder
Mr. Patrick Bowles, DLIAA Lawyer
Mr. Warren Hoy, DLIAA Secretary
Mrs. Mystery Chastain, DLIAA Treasurer
Mr. Otto Neely, DLIAA Board Member
Mr. Edward Moos, DLIAA Board Member
Mr. Richard Donovan, DLIAA Board Member
Mrs. Annette Scheibner, DLIAA Board Member
Mr. Walter Scurei, DLIAA Board Member at Large,
Mr. Everett Jordan, DLIAA Board Member at Large
The Scurei family, who donated the Berlin Wall Monument to DLIFLC
Ms. Tucker Hirsch, special contributor to this edition

TABLE OF CONTENTS

GENERAL
Acronyms used in this book	6
DLI - Its faculty and languages - Changing and growing	7
The graduates since 1941, in defense of their country	11
DLI, a vital national resource that should be preserved	19
DLI Crest and Rosetta Stone	22
Proficiency Levels: Listening, Reading, and Speaking, in short hand form	23

MY DLI AND VIETNAM EXPERIENCE
From DLI graduate in Vietnam to dean of every DLI school	25
Dean recalls experiences, lessons as DLIFLC student - "Attendance Attention, Application"	30
How DLI, the Army, and Vietnam taught me to succeed	36

EVOLUTION
The McNerney Years (1981-1985) - A time to build at DLIFLC	41
The evolution of Team Teaching at DLI - 1985 to 2005	49
Evolution of technology in the classroom, from 1947 to the present	57
Evolution of administrative and course development technology	64

THE BERLIN WALL MONUMENT
Berlin Wall finally arrives at DLI.	66
Berlin Wall dedication ceremony - Presidio of Monterey, 9 Nov 05	70

MEMORIAL DAY AND WAR ACCOUNTS
Memorial Day parade honors 13 DLIFLC graduates killed in action.	75
A tale of two linguists - An effort to rectify a Gulf War account.	80
DLIFLC responds to Operation Desert Shield linguistic needs.	84
DLIWC Graduates Killed as a Result of Hostile Action in Vietnam	86

LANGUAGE PROGRAMS
"Captain Blanco was here" - A brief account of DLI's Spanish program since the 1960s	88
Arabic Basic Course - Transition from 47 to 63 weeks	92
Arabic 63-week program proves successful	98
History of the Serbian/Croatian program at DLIFLC (1948 to1998)	100
Haitian Creole project - A real team effort	107

A brief account of DLI's Russian program since the 1970s.	111
"Hauptmann Schnell was Here" - A brief account of DLI's German program since the 1950s	118

PERSONALITIES

Early Army Language School Pioneer Alexander "Alex" Burz passes away	120
Alfie Tewfik Khalil, Union President (1947-2006)	122
Long ago and Nearby, the brief story of Alfred Galindo	124
Serge Issakow - Russian teacher, supervisor, chair, and dean	126
Han Yuan "Harry" Lee - Chinese teacher, tester, course developer, and chair	128
Grandson visits sea-going vet's grave at Presidio Cemetery.	130
Maria Baird, Spanish department teacher, supervisor, and chair.	132

HALL OF FAME

Hall of Fame Inductees 2006, 2007, and 2011	135

DLIAA-DLIF MERGER

DLI Alumni Association and DLI Foundation merger	148

ACRONYMS

ALS: Army Language School (1947-1963)
AM: Abdelmalek course
CHARLIE: Name given to the Viet Cong
CTS: Cryptological Training System
DLIFLC: Defense Language Institute Foreign Language Center
DLIAA: DLI Alumni Association (2001-2014)
DLIF: DLI Foundation (2011- Present)
DLPT: Defense Language Proficiency Test
DLAB: Defense Language Aptitude Battery
DLIEC: DLI East Coast Branch - DLIWC: DLI West Coast Branch
ELA: European and Latin American School
E1: European School I - E2: European School II
GITS: General Intelligence Training System
GO: Gulf to the Ocean Course
MSA: Modern Standard Arabic
MI: Military Intelligence – MIS: Military Intelligence Service
MISLS: Military Intelligence Service Language School
MTT: Mobile Training Team
POW: Prisoner of War
TRADOC: Training and Doctrine Command

Defense Language Institute campus in Monterey, California

GENERAL HISTORY
The Defense Language Institute
Its faculty and languages: Changing and growing
DLI 50th Anniversary *GLOBE* – November 1991

Many things impress the ordinary citizen when first getting acquainted with the Defense Language Institute. Among them are the number of languages taught, the number of students from all services, the impressive size of its faculty and the kaleidoscopic variety of nationalities.

This microcosm of the American melting pot has matured in more than 60 years to produce the most renowned language institution in the world. At one point DLI instructors taught more than 30 languages and dialects. In recent years international events and national security considerations have caused the Institute to consolidate to its present size. Currently (1991) several hundred faculty members from all corners of the globe teach more than 24 languages and three dialects.

The Institute started at the Presidio of San Francisco in 1941 as the Fourth Army Intelligence School when second-generation Americans of Japanese descent called Nisei-helped the nation by teaching Japanese to American soldiers. The U.S. Army recruited the instructors, mainly from the West Coast. Most of their early students were also Nisei.

The expanding importance of China and Korea during World War II led to the programming of one class of Chinese in February and one Korean in October 1945. Initially, minority communities in large cities such as San Francisco, Chicago and New York were the source of DLI instructors.

In the early 1940s the Institute moved to Camp Savage and then to Fort Snelling, Minn. In 1946 it relocated to the Presidio of Monterey to become the Army Language School and expanded significantly in the following two years, 1947-48.

As the preeminent leader in a post-World War II world, the U.S. military saw the importance of teaching the languages of its new friends and old enemies. Russian was introduced in 1947, followed by Chinese, Korean, French, Portuguese, Spanish, German, Greek, Turkish, and Persian-Farsi.

Spanish attracted its faculty from Mexico, Central and South America, and Spain. French drew its instructors from France, Belgium, Switzerland, Haiti and North Africa. Portuguese language teachers came from Portugal and Brazil.

The teaching of Arabic also began in 1947 with a faculty composed mainly of Iraqi immigrants. Later the Institute hired instructors of other Middle East nationalities, with Egyptians becoming the largest group. These Arabic instructors now teach Modern Standard Arabic as well as Egyptian, Levantine and Iraqi dialects. In 1948 came Albanian, Czech, Bulgarian, Danish, Swedish, Hungarian, Norwegian, Romanian, Polish, Serbo-Croatian and Slovenian.

Millions of professionals left the ruins of Europe and the Soviet Union during and after World War II, and some of them applied for and obtained language teaching positions at the Institute. The need for teachers of Chinese attracted immigrants from mainland China who had fled to Taiwan before and after the communist revolution. In the early 1950s immigrants from the Korean peninsula who had left a war-torn country joined the Korean faculty after the first several years of the fledgling Korean program.

More Asian languages were also added to the Institute's programs in the ensuing years. In the mid-fifties the school began teaching Burmese, Chinese-Cantonese, Vietnamese, Thai, Malay and Indonesian. Once again, recently arrived immigrants, this time from Asia, came to form a part of those early faculties.

During the same years, Finnish, Lithuanian, and Ukrainian were introduced.

In 1963 the Army Language School became the Defense Language Institute and began accepting members of all the military services. Several languages were also added in the last two decades: Dutch joined in the 1970s, drawing its instructors from the Netherlands. Hebrew, Tagalog, Dari and Pashto came in the 1980s. As many native born Americans as Israeli instructors taught Hebrew. Tagalog drew teachers from the Philippines, and the Dari/Pashto instructors came from Afghanistan. Presented another way, the historical picture of languages added to the DLI curriculum looks like the chart shown on the next page.

In the late 1980s, the teaching of a number of languages was discontinued at DLI. These languages, which included Albanian, Bulgarian, Chinese-Cantonese, Finnish, Hungarian, Indonesian, Malay, Lithuanian, Romanian, Serbian/ Croatian, Dari, Pashto, Norwegian, etc, continued to be taught on the East Coast by contract through the DLI Washington office. Teachers in those languages were either laid off, retired, went to teach other languages, or were employed in staff positions.

Four Presidio of Monterey buildings have been dedicated to faculty members. Nisei Hall, at this time home of the European and Latin American School, honors the Nisei pioneers. Munakata Hall, home of the Korean school, and the Aiso Library, were dedicated to the memories of Yukata Munakata and John Aiso, members of the first Japanese faculty. Munzer Hall honors Hans Munzer, a German scholar who spent his last few years working for DLI's System Development Agency in the 1970s.

The War on Terrorism, including the conflicts with Iraq and other problem spots, is switching U.S. interests from some languages to others, and no one knows what future impact these events will have on the Defense Language Institute. Certainly the learning of languages will continue to be of paramount importance to this country, and the American-and foreign-born faculty of DLI will continue making significant contributions.

Additions and deletions of languages from 1941 to 2015 are shown below:

	(+) ADDITIONS, (-) DELETIONS
1941	+ Japanese
1947	+ Chinese, Korean, Russian, Spanish, French, German + Portuguese, Greek, Turkish, Persian-Farsi, and Arabic
1948	+ Albanian, Czech/Slovak, Bulgarian, Danish, Swedish + Hungarian, Lithuanian, Norwegian, Romanian, Polish + Serbo-Croatian, and Slovenian
1950s	+ Burmese, Chinese-Cantonese, Vietnamese, Thai, Malay + Indonesian, German, Finish, Lithuanian, Ukrainian + Italian.
1960s	+ Swahili, Burmese - *Swahili, - Burmese*
1970s	+ Dutch
1980s	+ Hebrew, Tagalog, Dari, and Pashto - *Albanian, Bulgarian, Dari, Finnish, Hungarian, Indonesian,* - *Malay, Pashto, Romanian, Serbian/Croatian, Pashto,* - *Chinese-Cantonese, Norwegian*
1990s	+ Serbian/Croatian - *Dutch, Ukrainian, Slovak*
2001	- *Polish,*
2002	- *Czech*
2004	- *Greek*
2005	- *Vietnamese*
2014	- *Italian and Thai*
Post 9-11	+ Dari, Hindi, Pashto, Indonesian, Punjabi, Turkish, Urdu, and Uzbek

Presently, the eight DLI schools teach the following languages:

ASIAN SCHOOL 1: Chinese, Japanese, Tagalog
ASIAN SCHOOL 2: Korean
EUROPEAN AND LATIN AMERICAN SCHOOL: French, German, Hebrew, Portuguese, Russian, Spanish, and Serbian/Croatian,
MIDDLE EAST SCHOOL 1: MSA and Arabic Levantine dialect
MIDDLE EAST SCHOOL 2: MSA and Arabic Egyptian dialect
MIDDLE EAST SCHOOL 3: MSA and Arabic Egyptian & Sudanese dialects
MULTI-LANGUAGE SCHOOL: Dari, Hindi, Indonesian, Pashto, Punjabi, Turkish, Urdu, and Uzbek
PERSIAN SCHOOL: Persian-Farsi

DLIFLC Students, Faculty, and Staff at Soldier's Field, with the Monterey Bay in the background

The Graduates Since 1941
In defense of their country
DLI 50th Anniversary *GLOBE* – November 1991

"One of the most potent intelligence weapons ever known to humankind: Language"

Early on a Sunday several years ago, the man tending the recycling station in Seaside, California, was hanging up the OPEN sign while talking to an early customer. He complained that someone had tried to cheat him by putting a rock in a plastic bag of aluminum cans.

As my turn came, an Asian woman and her young daughter carried their load close to the recycling containers and waited. As he weighed my heap, the man turned to the women and began conversing with them in Vietnamese. Curious about his linguistic gift, I inquired, and he introduced himself. He said he was a former Vietnamese student of the Defense Language Institute (DLI) and a Special Forces soldier who had served in Vietnam in the mid-1960s.

He still remembered "Old Man Nguyen" and "Machine Gun Thiep" from the Vietnamese Department. He was, I realized, one of the forgotten thousands who in the last 60 years had passed through DLI to learn a language before going to war.

The forerunner of DLI, the Fourth Army Intelligence School, later called the Military Intelligence Service Language School, MISLS, was established at the Presidio of San Francisco on Nov. 1,

1941, five weeks before the United States entered World War II. The first language taught was Japanese to 60 second-generation Japanese soldiers. The history of the Nisei soldiers who graduated from MISLS in the early 1940s is well documented in DLI records, in the book *Yankee Samurai,* by Joseph Harrington (1979), and in the documentary film *The Color of Honor,* produced by Loni Ding.

The best-known MISLS graduates are the three World War II heroes for whom three DLI buildings are named: SGT George I. Nakamura, TSgt. Frank T. Hachiya, and TSGT Yukitaka Mizutari.

Numerous Japanese graduates of MISLS went on to perform heroic deeds in the Far East. They supplied the U.S. military with *one of the most potent intelligence weapons ever known to humankind: Language.*

Nisei military linguists in the Pacific Theater served as interpreters, interrogators and cave-flushers. They saved thousands of American lives and shortened the war by two years, according to GEN Charles Willoughby, MacArthur's G-2. Nisei Hall, the present home of Middle East School II, is named in their honor.

The School changed its location to Camp Savage in May 1942 and then to Fort Snelling, Minn., in August 1942. It remained a part of the Military Intelligence Service. Moving to Monterey, Calif., in the summer of 1946, it became the Army Language School (ALS), then the Defense Language Institute (DLI) in 1963, and then Defense Language Institute Foreign Language Center (DLIFLC) in 1975.

Since 1941 the School has grown considerably and now (1991) teaches 19 languages: Arabic, Chinese, Czech, French, German, Greek, Hebrew, Italian, Japanese, Korean, Persian, Portuguese, Serbian/Croatian, Spanish, Russian, Tagalog, Thai, Turkish, and Vietnamese.

Hundreds of MISLS and ALS Japanese language students did intelligence work during the Korean War at army, corps, division and regimental levels

The first MISLS/ALS casualty in the Korean War was SGT Funio Kido, a graduate with the 1st Cavalry near Pusan. Another soldier, SGT Frank Tokubo, took his 1st Reg., 1st Cav. Div. team of MISLS intelligence operatives all the way to the Yalu River. When the Chinese communist hordes attacked, Tokubo led his men back to Seoul, wading through icy rivers, over mountain passes and under constant attack by the Chinese

Pomerene Hall is named after CPT Robert Louis Pomerene, a 1949 graduate of the Russian language course who died as a result of wounds received in action Feb. 12, 1951 in Korea. Pomerene received the Silver Star posthumously for his actions that day.

Vietnam saw thousands of DLI graduates during the 10 years of the war. Since no effort was made to track them, not many can be identified at the present.

During my own tour in Vietnam in 1966-67, as a DLI graduate of French assigned to the 173rd Airborne Brigade, I only ran into three DLI graduates. The first, SGT Albert Rosenstine, had taken Spanish at DLI and was then assigned to the Interrogation Center of the Military Advisory Command, Vietnam, in Saigon. Rosenstine and I had attended together the interrogation course in Fort Holabird, Md.

The second, SSG Robert Destatte, a Vietnamese graduate, was my boss in the interrogation section of the MI Detachment, 173rd Airborne, in Bien Hoa, Vietnam. Destatte was such a good linguist that he could perform lengthy interrogations without any help from the Vietnamese interpreters and could converse with them for hours. By the time the war ended, Destatte had been in Vietnam four times, retiring as a warrant officer in 1980. He presently (1991) works for the Defense Intelligence Agency and has traveled to North Vietnam several times in connection with our efforts to identify the remains of MIAs. In recent years, he was has been keeping up his language skills through VTT from DLI instructors.

The name of the third graduate I can't remember. When I met him, he was interrogating for the "Bloody Red One." His linguistic talent was so impressive that, if they weren't looking at him, the Vietnamese couldn't tell he was not Vietnamese.

Bomar, Combs, Kendall, and Smith Halls are named after CPO Frank Willis Bomar, SFC Alfred H. Combs, GySgt George Percy Kendall, and SSG Herbert Smith, four DLI Vietnamese language graduates killed in action in the Republic of Vietnam in the late 1960s.

By any account, the most renowned DLI graduate during the Vietnam years is Col. James N. "Nick" Rowe, who, as a Special Forces lieutenant, took Chinese-Mandarin at DLI in the early 1960s.

After several months in Vietnam, Rowe was captured by the enemy and became the only officer during the war to be captured in South Vietnam by the Viet Cong. His five years as a prisoner of war are recounted in his book, *Five Years to Freedom (1971)*.

After leaving and then coming back to the Army, Rowe was again assigned to DLI -- as a student of Tagalog in August 1987, when I met him in my role as Dean of the Asian School. Rowe was proud of saying that his knowledge of Chinese helped him to survive in captivity, since many of the Viet Cong spoke Chinese as a second language. On March 18, 1988, when his Tagalog graduation and promotion to full colonel were celebrated in the former DLI Officers Club, one of his Chinese teachers, John Yuan, referred to him as a most dedicated student.

Upon graduation from the Tagalog course, Rowe departed for the Philippines. A year later he was gunned down by Filipino communist rebels, who had realized what a formidable adversary he was.

In 1967, during the Six Day War, the Naval Security Group sent an intelligence-gathering vessel, the USS *Liberty,* to the eastern Mediterranean to monitor communications. When war broke out, the American ship came under attack. Three-quarters of the crew were wounded or killed, including several Arabic linguists,

Col. Charles Scott studied Farsi at DLI in the early 1960s. On Nov. 4, 1979, while serving as head of the U.S. Army Mission to Iran at the American Embassy in Teheran, Scott was among the Americans seized and held hostage for 444 days.

During the Cold War, more than 100,000 DLI graduates served in field stations and military units around the world. Three Russian graduates who lost their lives during that era are MAJ Arthur D. Nicholson, Jr., CT13 Patrick R. Price, and Navy Lt. Robert F. Taylor.

Nicholson graduated from the Russian Basic Course in 1980. While working as a member of the U.S, Military Liaison Mission to the Group of Soviet forces in Germany, he was shot in East Germany by a Soviet sentry. Denied medical help, he bled to death. Price died in a 1987 aircraft accident on an operational mission, and Taylor was shot down by North Koreans in 1969 in an aircraft with more than 20 crew members -- all killed in action.

15 – Babel By The Bay

The United States involvement in the Lebanese civil war was a passive one. However, in October 1983, the bombing of the Marine barracks by a suicide attacker saw the deaths of 241 U.S. servicemen in one blast. Several DLI Arabic linguists were killed.

In 1980 the Department of Defense established the Rapid Deployment Joint Task Force to support contingency operations in the region. In 1982 the Army began to rotate infantry battalions into the Sinai Peninsula on peacekeeping duties with the Multinational Force and Observers. In 1985 several DLI graduates were killed when their fully loaded aircraft crashed in Gander, Newfoundland, while returning from duty in the Sinai.

During Operation Just Cause, no record was kept of DLI graduates who participated in the Panama invasion. However, we have knowledge of two DLI linguists who went to assist in translating and interrogating. One, SSG Joseph B. Butin, an Arabic student who was already a Spanish linguist, was pulled out of the Arabic course and sent to Panama with a few hours' notice. The other was SFC J.B. Quinn, senior Military Language Instructor in the European and Latin American School. Both soldiers served in the headquarters of the SOUTHCOM commander in chief, GEN. Maxwell Thurman.

The invasion of Kuwait by Saddam Hussein gave DLI graduates an opportunity to again prove their worth. By the end of August 1990, hundreds of them had deployed with the largest American expeditionary force in recent history. A group of them served with the 311th MI battalion, "The Eye of the Eagle," of the renowned "Screaming Eagles," the 101st Airborne Division (Air Assault). Another group left for Saudi Arabia from Utah with the Army National Guard's 142nd MI Battalion, and another from Fort Bragg with the 519th MI Battalion.

The first Army casualty in Saudi Arabia was LT Tommie Bates of the 24th Infantry Division (Mechanized), a DLI graduate of Greek. On Sept. 14, 1990, Bates was killed in a vehicle accident in Dahran. SGT Lee A. Belas, a 1989 Russian graduate, was killed in action on 27 February 1991 during Operation Desert Storm when his helicopter was shot down by Iraqi ground fire. The dining facility "Belas Hall" was named after him.

News releases and letters received by Arabic instructors from those graduates construct an interesting picture of linguist use during the Persian Gulf War. CPT Robert Bush (DL1-'85') wrote:

"Remember on the news about the six Iraqi prisoners of war? When they were transferred from the front and brought to the POW camp, guess who settled them down and all in Arabic? Yes! Little old me. Everyone said I did a good job. Very first time with POWs."

SPC Michael Landolfi's main weapon was not an M-16. It was a mega-phone. From an Apache helicopter gunship, the lanky, bespectacled soldier convinced 450 Iraqi soldiers to surrender after telling them they would be slaughtered if they didn't give up.*

Sergeant James Phipps said he processed an enemy prisoner of war who waited to be treated for an old wound received during the Iran-Iraq war.

SPC Jennie Lynn Deitz, wrote from Saudi Arabia, *". . . just by [my] using the Iraqi greeting, SHLONAK, the [Iraq] prisoners seemed to relax. Many showed me pictures of their families and were at ease just chatting about their lives outside of the Army. The majority of the prisoners enjoyed talking to females. This made my job as an interrogator much easier."*

DLI Military Language Instructors and platoon sergeants were taken from their DLI assignments to join the war effort. GySgt Terry Parrish, MSgt. Doug Daniels, SFC Morley Curtis, SFC Daniel Tully, SFC Kirk Oakley, and GySgt Michael Snell were all assigned to combat units and contributed to the coalition victory with their language expertise.

However the most celebrated Arabic graduate during operation Desert Shield/ Storm was Air Force Maj. Rick Francona. Francona went through Arabic basic and intermediate in the late 1970s. He later became technical language assistant in the Arabic program, performing these duties for two years.

After becoming a career intelligence officer, Francona served in Baghdad as a liaison officer to Iraqi military intelligence in 1988. He rose to the rank of major and during the Gulf War was assigned to Army Central Command in Saudi Arabia as one of the

---

* Years later this story was set right by Landolfi (See "A Tale of two Linguists - An effort to rectify a Gulf War account," on page 80 of this book)

interpreters of GEN Norman Schwarzkopf. Francona was often asked to brief high-ranking Arabic officers and to translate for American generals. He was present during the meetings between Schwarzkopf and the Iraqis to negotiate the cessation of hostilities. On his recent trips to Monterey, Francona has addressed all the Arabic students and all the DLI Foreign Area Officers, giving a first-hand account of his experiences. Francona is now retired and has written a book *Ally to Adversary, An Eyewitness Account of Iraq's Fall from Grace (1999)*".

Gen. Norman Schwarzkopf with his interpreter, AF Major Rick Francona, DLI graduate of the Basic and Intermediate Arabic courses, and later Arabic MLI. - Iraq, March 1991

The only known DLI graduate in Africa was SGT Kenneth R. Hobson, a 1993 Arabic graduate, who was killed in embassy bombing in Nairobi, Kenya, 1998. The "Hobson Recreation Center" was named after him.

In the 1990s, many DLI graduates again served their country in faraway places like Kuwait, Saudi Arabia, Haiti and the Balkans. In the mid 90's some of the DLI graduates from a conversion course (from French to Haitian-Creole) ended pulling duties in the Caribbean island.

The great majority of graduates serving in the Balkan Peninsula were Russian and Serbian/Croatian linguists. For example, SSG Kevin Johnson, an Arabic, Russian and Serbian/ Croatian (short course) linguist served in both Kuwait and Bosnia. In Kuwait he found interesting the eating rituals of the common folk and the importance of knowing one's right from the left hand. In his first encounter with Bosnians he thanked DLI for having taught him sports vocabulary, as the first time he spoke to almost any Bosnian, they began the conversation talking about the soccer game that was on TV the night before.

Navy Senior Chief Mitch Murphy, another Serbian/Croatian graduate pulled duties in Bosnia as a translator for Admiral Leighton Smith, Commander of NATO Implementation Force in Bosnia from Dec 95 to Jun 96. He also translated for U.S. Secretary of State Madeleine Albright, UN Secretary Kofi Annan, and for the presidents and foreign ministers of several Balkan republics. Working with the Navy Seals, Murphy did recon work for all the Admiral visits. One of his assignments in 1996 was to visit an encampment suspected to be a death camp. When he arrived at the place with two Navy Seals, a couple of Bosnian Serb guards, armed with AK47s refused them entrance to the camp. Through skillful use of Serbian Croatian, mixed with threats that high ranking military officers would show up the following day with War Crimes Tribunal personnel, the guards allowed Murphy and the Seals in. In fact, inside they found an entire brigade of Bosnian Serbs and clear evidence of a mass grave and Death Camp for Bosnian Moslems.

The terrorist bombings in New York and Washington will definitely impact on the utilization of linguists in the armed forces, and as generations of DL1 graduates continue passing through the language pipeline, potential celebrities and heroes await their opportunity to honor the Defense Language Institute by contributing to their country with a unique expertise. ❖

DLIFLC Crest

DLI, a vital national resource that should be preserved

DLIAA Newsletter VI – April 2005

The Defense Language Institute (DLI) is a valuable national resource that should be preserved. From its modest beginnings on the eve of World War II at the Presidio of San Francisco to its enterprising present at the Presidio of Monterey, DLI has been a premier language institution in two very important senses -- it has provided the United States military with one of the most potent intelligence weapons ever known to humankind: language, and the Monterey campus has offered the largest concentration of language professionals experts in the world since 1947. In the last six decades, through a systematic and well-organized program, the Defense Language Institute has consistently produced linguists capable of using their newly acquired language to gather intelligence on land, air and sea. Whether assigned to Army infantry units, Navy ships, Marine battalions or Air Force aircraft, DLI graduates have proven their worth. In the Gulf War, even graduates who were principally trained as listeners were called on to work as interrogators, interpreter, and translators, demonstrating that their knowledge of the basic language was well-grounded.

Our very first graduates, second generation Japanese-Americans, Nisei, fought with brains and bullets in the Pacific Theater. Owing to their efforts, World War II was shortened by two years, said Gen Charles Willoughby, a member of Gen Douglas Macarthur's staff. Their skills, applied while island hopping and soldiering with the rest of our World War II heroes, were instrumental in communicating, translating, and interpreting for the surrender of the Japanese high command.

One of the most historic feats was the interception and translation of the Japanese military code. According to Bill Wagner, writing for the VFW Magazine *"The Nisei's biggest intelligence coup was the capture and translation of the Z Plan, Imperial Japan's strategy for defending the Marianas Islands (Guam and Saipan). Armed with that translation, Adm. Raymond Spruance's pilots destroyed Japanese air bases and scores of aircraft before the landings. Another coup was the Imperial Japanese army's ordnance inventory. It listed amounts, types and manufacturer's names and locations on the home islands, providing new targets for B-29s."* "The Nisei soldiers" served from the icy tundra of Kiska and Attu in Alaska's Aleutians to the boiling jungles of Burma and India, and on still classified missions with the OSS, Office of Strategic Services, a CIA forerunners."

Since those historic days, military linguists, the great majority graduates of the Defense Language Institute, have fought and died alongside their comrades in the frozen hills of Korea and the steaming jungles of Vietnam. And again, they started at the face of combat in war-torn Beirut, where 241 marines died in the explosion of the Marine barracks; in besieged Panama, where they communicated on the spot with the native population; and in the desolate vastness of sun-scorched Arabia, where between sun, sweat, and sand they patiently waited for the 100-hours war, and where one of them became the personal interpreter for Gen Schwarzkopf. They were also in Somalia, and later tried their language skills in Bosnia and Kosovo. More recently, many have served more than once in Iraq and Afghanistan, assisting commanders with the difficult task of understanding the local cultures. Additionally, scores of unsung heroes graduated from DLI during the five decades of the cold war, many spending endless hours in listening posts, ready to detect the actions and intentions of

American foes. However, the greatest exploits of our linguist heroes are unfortunately shrouded in the secrecy of their intelligence work. Demonstration of this secrecy is the fact that some of the accomplishments of the Nisei were still classified in the 1970s.

While acquiring their language, DLI students have interacted with the highest concentration of language experts in the world, their civilian teachers. These foreign-born professionals have constituted the first contact the students have had with foreign cultures. Thus, for six decades American military students have been exposed directly and indirectly to verbal and non-verbal behavioral patterns that, once understood, have given them powerful insights into other cultures' logic and ways of thinking.

This pool of extraordinary professionals was not created overnight. After the initial wave of Nisei instructors came a stream of professionals from Europe, Latin America, the Middle and the Far East beginning in 1947 and continuing today. Immigrants from all the corners of the globe have enlightened and enriched the intellect of several generations of servicemen and women.

In 60 plus years, the DLI organization has matured, solidified, and evolved into a cohesive force capable of meeting the language challenges of the twenty-first century. Its 900 plus foreign language teachers represent a powerful intellectual force impossible to duplicate without considerable time, effort and expense. The Defense Language Institute is definitely a valuable national resource that should be preserved. No other institution presently exists that can replicate the DLI's accomplishments of the last 60 some years, and conceivable it could take many years before another comparable organization can be created to fill its shoes. Never in the history of military intelligence have so few trained so many to understand so much in so many languages.

❖

DLI Crest   Reduced version of Rosetta Stone

DLI Crest and Rosetta Stone
DLIAA Newsletter VII – July 2005

The following quote is from the DLI Catalog:

"The Institute's Crest symbolizes the dual heritage of the Defense Language Institute and the Presidio of Monterey. Originally designed for the U.S. Army Language School, the crest was adopted in 1963 by the Defense Language Institute. It is also used by our sister school, the Defense Language Institute English Language Center.

The upper right corner of the shield depicts a fragment of the Rosetta Stone bearing the name of Egyptian ruler Ptolemy V (203–181 BC) in two languages (ancient Egyptian and Greek) and three scripts (Egyptian hieroglyphic and demotic scripts and Greek capital letters). Its discovery by a French military expedition in 1799 enabled scholars for the first time to decipher this complex pictographic writing, from which much of our knowledge of Egypt's ancient civilization is derived."

The cap on the lower left portion was worn by the San Carlos Catalan Volunteers, Spanish soldiers who accompanied Father Junipero Serra on his Sacred Expedition of 1769–70 to establish a string of missions in Alta California. In 1770, on the site of present-day Monterey, they built a small fort (presidio) to protect the San Carlos Borromeo Mission. Red and blue reflect the wartime and peacetime missions of the Institute, and the green olive branch reflects the aim of promoting peace through understanding. The gold torch on top is a traditional symbol of learning and knowledge."

❖

PROFICIENCY LEVELS
Listening, Reading, and Speaking in short hand form

LEVEL 1 LISTENING	LEVEL 1 - READING	LEVEL 1 SPEAKING
CAN GET THE MAIN IDEA WHEN LISTENING TO: • Statements about basic survival needs (meals, lodging, time, transportation, simple directions) • Simple questions and answers • Route instructions	CAN GET SOME MAIN IDEAS WHEN READING: • Simple narratives of routine actions • Simple descriptions of people, places and things • Simple explanations intended for tourists	CAN PARTICIPATE IN SIMPLE CONVERSATIONS THAT INCLUDE: • Introductions, exchange of greetings, and minimum courtesy requirements • Predictable personal and accommodations needs • Asking and answering questions • Simple biographical information • Explaining routine procedures

LEVEL 1+ LISTENING	LEVEL 1+ READING	LEVEL 1+ SPEAKING
CAN GET THE MAIN IDEA & SOME FACTS WHEN LISTENING TO: • Short conversations about basic survival needs • Brief social conversations • Simple discourse	CAN GET SOME MAIN IDEAS AND ESSENTIAL POINTS WHEN READING: • Announcements • Simple narration of events • Simple biographical information • Social notices • Straightforward	CAN INITIATE AND MAINTAIN PREDICTAPLE CONVERSATIONS THAT INCLUDE: • Travel and accommodation needs • Limited social demands • Very limited descriptions

LEVEL 2 LISTENING	LEVEL 2 READING	LEVEL 2 SPEAKING
CAN UNDERSTAND THE FACTS WHEN LISTENING TO: • Descriptions • Narrations of past, present and future events • Conversations about everyday topics • Personal and family news • Well-known current events • Routine office matters	CAN LOCATE AND UNDERSTAND MAIN IDEAS AND DETAILS WHEN READING: • Simple factual, familiar materials • Descriptions and narrations of repeatedly occurring events • Simple biographical information • Social notices • Formulaic business letters; • Simple	CAN PARTICIPATE IN EXTENSIVE CASUAL CONVERSATIONS ABOUT WORK, FAMILY AND CURRENT EVENTS: • Can ask/answer predictable questions at work • Can give complicated detailed directions • Can make non-routine changes and arrangements • Can describe and narrate in the past, present, and future
LEVEL 2+ LISTENING	LEVEL 2+ READING	LEVEL 2+ SPEAKING
CAN UNDERSTAND THE FACTS, + SOME IMPLICATIONS AND EMOTIONAL OVERTONES, WHEN LISTENING TO: • Most routine and social conversations • Most work related conversations • Some concrete discussions in a	CAN LOCATE & UNDERSTAND THE MAIN IDEA AND MOST FACTS, WHEN READING: • Factual, nontechnical prose • Some concrete discourse in professional field • Can make sensible guesses about unfamiliar material	SPEAKING – CAN PARTICIPATE IN MOST SOCIAL, FORMAL AND INFORMAL INTERACTIONS: • Can satisfy most work requirements • Can communicate effectively in specialized field

Ben De La Selva and J. Cherba in Dakto, Vietnam, 1967

MY DLI AND VIETNAM EXPERIENCE

From DLI graduate in Vietnam to dean of every DLI school

DLI *GLOBE* – October 1992

Memories of the French Language course at the Defense Language Institute were faint in my mind when I reported to the 173rd Airborne Brigade (Separate) in Vietnam in August 1966.

There, under a half-covered field tent, a master sergeant began his orientation by dispensing threats and obscenities to us, scared troops who had just arrived from the 90th Replacement Detachment, where we had been held for several days after an exhaustive plane trip from California. After handing each of us a manila folder that read, "THE 173RD AIRBORNE BRIGADE WELCOMES YOU TO VIETNAM," he narrated the brigade's history from its arrival in 1965 from Okinawa to the latest field operations, including the number of casualties and the amount of captured equipment. He dramatized the dangers of staying in the nearby town of Bien Hoa after curfew and told us stories of live grenades thrown inside crowded bars and of dead troopers brought back to the base camp wrapped in mattress covers.

This was not where I expected to be a year earlier when, as an Army specialist, I entered the French language course at DLI. But my fate became evident when I was sent to the Prisoners-of War (POW) interrogation course in Fort Holabird, Md., the predecessor of Fort Huachuca, AZ. In August 1966, without fanfare, I made the 22-hour flight from Travis Air Force Base (AFB) to Saigon via Braniff 747—with only one stop in Clark AFB, Republic of Philippines. On the plane I reflected that DLI had done its best to prepare me for my linguistic work and the Army had made me a soldier. It was time to get to work.

SPC Dale Harwood drove me from the 90th Replacement Detachment to the Military Intelligence Detachment area, where I reported for duty at the Interrogation of Prisoners of War (IPW) Section. A major commanded the detachment, which had about the same number of officers as enlisted men. Soon I was introduced to everyone in the IPW section, the Order of Battle (OB) and the Imagery Interpretation (II) sections. During the first several days I found it nearly impossible to sleep. Helicopters flew overhead day and night, and artillery fire went on relentlessly. In the detachment area, the troopers had constructed makeshift shelters with sand bags as protection against mortar attacks. After all, our base was also known as "Rocket City" for the numerous mortar and rocket attacks endured during the previous year. Inside the base camp were other dangers. Troops returning from town at night found themselves exposed to Claymore mines, set up by Vietcong sympathizers who came to the base camp under the guise of kitchen helpers, hired hands, and laborers.

The main body of the MI detachment always accompanied Brigade headquarters to every field operation. Sometimes transported by air, the brigade often traveled by convoy and frequently encountered sniper fire from both sides of the road. The MI Detachment's mission was to gather intelligence through interrogation of prisoners and the capture of enemy documents, materials and weapons. Back in the base camp, members of the I I (eye eye) Section accomplished that mission by examining hundreds of photos taken by U.S. aircraft to scan terrain patterns, detect enemy movements and identify ideal terrain for airborne drop zones.

A group of Vietnamese interpreters and interrogators commanded by a Vietnamese captain who proudly wore the sobriquet, "Diablo," augmented the detachment. After fire fights, paratrooper "grunts" would bring suspected Vietcong to the detachment area, where one of us would go through routine questioning procedures: "Where was the prisoner captured?" "What was he doing at the time of capture?" "Was he carrying weapons?" "What was the prisoner's attitude?" The prisoner was then taken into a secure area and thoroughly interrogated in one of three ways: In English through a Vietnamese interpreter, directly in Vietnamese by a Vietnamese interrogator, or by a Vietnamese linguist (a rarity) with or without the help of an interpreter. After interrogation reports were completed using an old manual typewriter, the prisoners were sent to a higher headquarters area for disposition.

Wounded Vietcong who were not brought to us directly were taken to field hospitals. There we interrogated them while they lay under sedation --one time as doctors amputated the prisoner's arm. At other times we had the unpleasant duty of undressing dead soldiers because the Saigon Interrogation Center needed their uniforms.

The IPW section comprised a captain, a lieutenant, an Non Commissioned Officer In Charge (NCOIC) and several interrogators. My job as NCOIC ended in December upon the arrival of SSG Robert Destatte, a Vietnamese linguist who had graduated from DLI a few years earlier and had already spent a tour in Vietnam. I watched, amazed, to see this American soldier get along so well with the Vietnamese. He not only spoke fluent Vietnamese, but gained their trust from the very beginning by showing respect for their ways of doing things which were often at odds with ours. Destatte, needless to say, interrogated in Vietnamese. Clearly, his cultural awareness, however acquired, was crucial to his success as an interrogator and as an unwitting American ambassador in that faraway land. Thorough and systematic, he combined technical and language skills to do a decent and efficient job. He saw to it that prisoners were processed, interrogated, fed, and transported with diligence. He made sure to read and translate documents and itemize and package materials expeditiously. Under his supervision, we identified, catalogued, and periodically took weapons to Saigon, and transported captured grenades and claymore mines to ordnance disposal units.

The Brigade published periodic letters and sent them to all troopers. On March 18, 1967, we received a congratulatory letter from the brigade commander, Brigade General John R. Deane Jr. that read, in part, *"Operation Junction City marked another first for the 173rd Airborne Brigade (Separate), as members of the Brigade conducted the first combat jump by U.S. forces in Vietnam."*

The jump and subsequent heliborne assaults on Feb 22, 1967, demonstrated your professionalism at its best."

Although we did not make that historic jump, members of our interrogation team arrived at the drop zone at daybreak and saw a sea of parachutes on the ground and several hanging from trees. The operation resulted in 266 enemy killed in action and dozens of enemy prisoners taken.

Was I sent to Vietnam as a French linguist? Probably not. I met many soldiers in intelligence jobs who had learned Spanish, Polish, Russian and other languages at DLI; however, the fact that most middle class Vietnamese spoke French came in handy for me.

The French had been in Vietnam more than 100 years and officially departed in 1954 after their defeat in Dien Bien Phu. So it didn't surprise us to find French priests in many villages. I put my French to use for the first time when the brigade went into a village the day after the Vietcong had kidnapped all its young males. We considered the French priest a source of information, and I had to question him. I felt proud of the fact that I gathered information on the Vietcong moves and thanked my DLI teachers. Two months after the 173rd moved north Central Highlands, I returned to the U.S. -- right before the famous battle of Dakto. I left Vietnam on August 26, 1967, the same day I had arrived a year earlier.

As DLI student of French, I never thought I'd end up in Vietnam as a POW interrogator, but I was probably one of the earliest graduates to have served in Vietnam. After one year of hardships my blessings doubled when, at the end of my tour, I received orders to report again to DLI - this time to tackle Polish, the language I studied hard through my last days in the Army in the spring of 1968.

After leaving the service, I stayed away from the military for several years, but came back to DLI as a civilian to work in the

Systems Development Agency, where I participated in the writing of the Spanish basic course.

The following decade saw me in almost every DLI directorate, including 1 1/2 years as programs manager in the Provost office. In the mid 1980's I became dean to the then combined Asian and Korean Schools. In 1989 I was transferred to the combined Middle East Schools and from 1993 to the present I served as dean in European I, European II, and the European and Latin American School. Thus, from 1985 to 1991 I served as dean of every school at DLI.

I hope that my career, which began as a DLI student, is an encouragement to current students, who may come back to be school deans someday. ❖

With friends at the snack bar "Stammtisch. Front row: Irene Baratoff, Rene De Barros, Ben De La Selva, and Dennis Leatherman. Back row: Alex Burz, Joseph Rosa, Howard Rowland, and Nick Itsines, ," circa 2005. ❖

Fleur de Lis Polish Eagle

Dean recalls experiences, lessons as DLIFLC student
"Attendance, Attention, Application"
Adapted from a DLI *GLOBE* article - December 1997

Although, presently the dean of the European and Latin American School, my first contact with the Defense Language Institute dates back to November 1965 when as a soldier I arrived at the Presidio of Monterey to take the 24-week French Basic Course in Nisei Hall. After the French course I attended the Prisoners of War Interrogator's course at Fort Holabird, Md., the precursor of Fort Huachuca. The orders I received in August 1966 at Holabird assigned me to the Military Intelligence detachment, 173rd Airborne Brigade (Separate), Republic of Vietnam, at a camp near the town of Bien Hoa.

I was assigned to the Prisoners of War Section and with them accompanied the brigade headquarters on nearly every "search and destroy" operation from Aug. 26, 1966, to July 1967. All but one of the members in the Prisoner of War Section interrogated only in English using Vietnamese interpreters. Even so, as there was usually a French priest in most villages, my DLI training in French came in handy. Also, almost every middle class Vietnamese spoke French fluently because the French had been in Vietnam nearly 150 years and had only left in 1954.

MI Detachment, 173rd Airborne Brigade, Bien Hoa, Vietnam, 1966

One day near the end of my tour, I received my rotation orders dated July 26, 1967, assigning me back to the continental United States. That day, under a prisoner's tent in Dakto, Central Highlands, shirtless and sweaty after a long day of interrogation with the help of the Montagnards, I found out that I was going back to DLI. My orders read in part: "... report to Company B, Defense Language Institute, West Coast Branch, for training in Polish class 01PL47W0268."

I left Vietnam Aug. 26, 1967, and after a short leave in San Francisco, I showed up at the Presidio in September 1967 and reported to Company B orderly room. In all honesty, I did not want to study Polish. While in Vietnam I had gone on Rest and Recuperation leave to Japan and wanted to study Japanese to get myself assigned there. Sure that I could have the language changed, I visited the military personnel officer to tell him that if he did not switch me to Japanese, I would not reenlist. After listening to my story, without hesitating the personnel officer picked up the phone and tried to contact the Department of the Army to have my language training canceled and to reassign me someplace else. When I saw that my bluff wasn't working, I told him that I was willing to take Polish, and with a smile he put the phone down.

At that time, DLI students taking Slavic languages had their barracks on Soldier Field. There were 16 wooden barracks that had been built in 1942 and covered the entire field in pairs from the Soldier Field Parade Stand down to Patton Avenue. On the Kit Carson Road side sat two square wooden buildings containing the mess halls and two supply rooms. The classrooms were located to the north and south of the field. Russian and Serbian-Croatian were taught in the buildings between the post theater and the NCO -- now the Edge -- Club, buildings 209 through 218. Polish, Czech, Hungarian, and other East European languages were taught on the opposite side of the field, in buildings 272 through 275.

The DLI headquarters was housed in building 276. My barracks sat across the street from building 212. Every weekday we would fall out for reveille formation on that narrow street parallel to 15th Infantry Street. East European language students lived in my barracks, and the population was multi-service. The senior serviceman -- only men lived in the barracks -- regardless of service, became the platoon non-commissioned officer.

Since my Polish class did not begin until November, there was not much for me to do on post. I spent my days in the library, supervising details, or in town. Finally, November arrived and during the student orientation, I discovered that one of my teachers, Gabrielle Lubomirski, was the wife of one of my former French instructors. He had already told her I had been an exemplary student. At the orientation we were issued a dozen books, a reel-to-reel tape recorder weighing about 30 pounds, and about 20 tapes. Polish came easily to me except for the sounds SZ and CZ, especially when they came together, as in JESZCZE, "yet", "still". The late 60s was the heyday of the Audio Lingual method at DLI.

At the beginning of the course we were not allowed to see the Polish script. As mnemonic aides, students came up with their own phonetic system to represent the Polish sounds. It wasn't until weeks after the beginning that we started to read in Polish. Lessons were arranged by topics and grammatically sequenced so as to cover the seven cases in a certain order: Nominative, Accusative, Dative, Genitive, Locative, Vocative and Instrumental. Each lesson contained a dialogue and a reading passage, plus pattern drills, lab exercises and homework assignments. The new lesson of the day was introduced during the second hour in the afternoon which was spent on perception drills. Using the inductive method, instructors would introduce pattern drills to us exemplifying a certain grammatical point, expecting that from the examples we students would figure out the under-lying rule. At the end of the patterns, the instructor might or might not give us the rule. During the last hour of each day, instructors introduced a dialogue containing the patterns of the previous hour. The dialogue had to be learned by heart in the evening with the help of the reel-to-reel tape recorder. The rest of the homework consisted mainly of listening to recorded questions about the dialogue and answering those questions in writing. The first hour of the following morning consisted of reciting the dialogue verbatim, with the instructor making corrections at the end. During the second hour, we covered the reading passage, reading it aloud, translating it and getting whatever cultural information was contained in it or in the dialogue. The third hour was spent on pattern drills, practicing those features already presented. The first hour in the afternoon was left for guided or free conversation that began with the lesson topic and worked itself around to topics of personal interest. The cycle began again during the second afternoon hour.

As the course proceeded, it began to take more than one day to go through one lesson because by then the instructors had to make time for many more other activities relating to the lesson core. In addition, once every two weeks the whole department would meet in the basement of building 274 to sing Polish songs, accompanied by Waclaw Bevensee or Zbigniew Palucki's piano playing. I still remember some of them like "Serce w Plecaku." It is interesting to note that authentic materials were almost non-existent, and the ones we got, like newspapers, magazines and Voice of America tapes, were at least six to eight months old. The Audio-Lingual method lesson cycle was deadly and, just as now, we students became bored with the daily routine, although we managed to keep at it and didn't let the boredom get the best of us. Many other problems we encountered have not changed in 30 years either. We complained about bad English on tests, tests that contained information never seen before, changing grading schemes, tapes with static, lots of homework, teachers' coordination, and so on. However, we realized by talking to students in other languages that the quality of our Polish instruction was first rate.

The department was headed by Dr. Stefan Kaminski. The Polish course developer was Dr. Tadeusz Haska, who in later years also became chair. At that time Haska was commuting to the University of California, Berkeley, to obtain his doctorate. My main instructor we were told was a countess by birth and a princess by marriage. Other instructors who came often to my classes were Dr. Józef Kasparek-Obst, Zygmunt Wolf, Bevensee, Palucki, Zygmunt Shumelda, Jan Truskolaski, Tadeusz Rudiger, Maciej Radziwill, of noble origin and whose cousin had married Jackie Kennedy's sister; Kazimierz Gonet and Edward Wodecki. The last two were also proficient in Russian and were sent back and forth between the Russian and Polish programs to balance the number of instructors in each program. Other instructors who taught in the department before my time were Zygmunt Wasowski and Wladyslaw Grzymala-Siedlecki. These instructors formed a solid and competent language teaching group.

As Polish came easily to me, I was motivated enough to seek other ways to improve my proficiency. For example, I only spoke in Polish to the instructors. The thing that did the most for me, however, started when I discovered that in the barracks there was a very talented student -- whose name I don't remember -- who was also studying Polish but who was ahead of me by several weeks. This young man and I swore we would only talk to each other in Polish, whether on or off post. So we would go out to town and never use English. One night at the restaurant La Fonda, two young women began laughing when they heard us talking in Polish at the bar. They were second generation Poles on vacation from Chicago. We drove them around the Monterey Peninsula and even invited them to visit the Polish Department. Another thing that really helped me in my studies was that I never missed a class. I had a perfect attendance record in French, and ended up the same way in Polish. I became a Cal Ripken of sorts. Even after a rough weekend, when I felt like going on sick call and not to class, I forced myself to walk from the barracks and across Soldier Field to building 274, to my classroom, located where Pam Taylor of Academic Administration have their offices now.

During class I was never distracted by either teachers' mannerisms or by disagreeing with the department's methodology. Without being conscious of it, somehow I knew the moment I began to dwell on matters outside of my learning Polish, that was the moment my learning would slow down or stop. Distractions included problems with my military unit and with the other students. Somehow, I did not take those problems personally. Another positive thing was I never failed to turn in my home-work. Besides memorizing a long dialogue, which I soon learned from the printed page without listening to the reel-to-reel tape, we were asked to listen to passages and answer the recorded questions in writing. Often we turned in compositions related directly or indirectly to the topic of the lesson. These compositions were immediately corrected

I was a successful student, but I really did not realize why until many years later when I read a Sunday newspaper supplement containing an article titled: *"Asian Kids, Why do They Excel?"* The formula was there and, put simply it amounted to: "Go to class every day; pay attention in class, apply yourself." In three words: *"Attendance, Attention and Applica-tion."* I left DLI and the Army in 1968, used the GI Bill in San Jose to acquire a college degree and came back to DLI in 1972 as a Spanish course developer and instructor. Thereafter, I worked my way up to school dean. I became dean of the combined Asian I and Asian II schools in 1985, dean of the combined Middle East I and Middle East II schools in 1989, dean of European School II in 1993, dean of European School I in 1996, and dean of my present school in 1998. As I look back over my DLI career since 1965, I realize I might be the only employee in its history to have worked in every one of its schools. With all that background, the best advice I give incoming students during orientation is *"Attendance, Attention, Application,"* a formula for success in any learning endeavor.

❖

How DLI, the Army, and Vietnam taught me to succeed

DLI *GLOBE* –January 2005

I was born and raised in the town of Somoto, Nicaragua; a town of about 2,000 souls with one of the worst school systems in the world, and so insignificant it did not appear on maps. The town had no college, high school, or library, and was located practically in the middle of nowhere. Sometimes I think that my last name, De La Selva (from the jungle), was made up to fit that reality. I came to the United States in my early twenties and six months later joined the US Army. What follows is my personal story.

Last year, I was a DLI school dean and ready to retire after 40 years of federal service. However, my first contact with the Institute dates back to 1965 when as a soldier I arrived at DLI to take the French basic course. The French department was then situated in Nisei Hall and was directed by a former diplomat by the name of Piccard. Among the instructors were Messrs. Lubomirski, Bouassu, Courrealt, Villani, and Ceriez; and also Mesdames Low, Redmon, Nguyen, and Tournier. My barracks were located within walking distance, where the Navy Detachment is presently located.

After 24 weeks of French I attended the Army Prisoners of War Interrogator's course in Fort Holabird, Maryland, where I received orders assigning me to the Military Intelligence detachment, 173rd Airborne Brigade, in Bien Hoa, Vietnam, a camp near Saigon.

I flew to Vietnam with 200 other soldiers on a purple 747. The 22 hours long flight started at Travis Air Force Base, Calif., and made only one stop in the Philippines. Shortly before arriving at Tan Son Nhut Airport, the announcement came from the pilot that we would be landing in a few minutes. I had traveled by air many times but this time the jerky twists and turns of the airplane and a sudden dive made me and everyone else very nervous. Someone on my left knelt down and began praying until he was forced to buckle up. Another soldier threw up, missing the paper bag.

Once the airplane landed and the door was opened, a gust of hot air hit my face and a strange smell hit my nostrils. To this day I still remember that smell when I use weed killer in my garden. It was the smell of defoliant, used by the military to kill vegetation. The exit from that airplane was the entrance to Hell for many on the airplane. At that moment, I wondered how many of us on that airplane would be returning home to the United States of America a year later.

No longer after a short drive to the 90th Replacement Detachment, we got in line to get a pair of sheets for the night – they did not issue blankets in Vietnam. The soldier issuing the sheets said that there had been a mortar attack the night before and that he had only three days left in Vietnam. Jokingly, I volunteered to exchange places with him.

The following day a paratrooper picked me up and I was on my way to join the 173rd Airborne Brigade, an infantry unit whose main mission was to guard the Bien Hoa air base. Soon I was initiated in the Prisoner of War Interrogation Section. I spent a few days watching American soldiers questioning suspects and refugees through Vietnamese interpreters.

With the MI detachment, I accompanied the brigade headquarters on nearly every "Search and Destroy" operation from August 1966 to August 1967. Most members in the Prisoner of War Section interrogated in English through Vietnamese interpreters. However, as there was usually a French priest in most villages, my DLI training in French came in handy. Additionally, most middle class Vietnamese spoke French since the French had been in Vietnam nearly 150 years and had only left after the battle of Dien Bien Phu, in 1954.

My Vietnam tour was a mix of fear and boredom. During the first two weeks, I was unable to sleep, such was the noise from artillery fire and helicopters leaving and arriving 24 hours a day. In the base camp, or rear area, we were exposed to claymore mines that unexpectedly exploded while driving to the nearby villages. In bars frequented by our troops, the Vietcong, also given the friendly name of Charlie, would throw grenades inside the bars and then take off, leaving dozen of dead and wounded GIs. Soldiers who spent the night with bar girls often were brought back wrapped in mattress covers, dead. And religiously, every day at 7 a.m., the Armed Forces radio began its morning broadcasting with someone bellowing: *"Good Morning, Vietnam."*

During Search and Destroy operations we would approach a town where all the young men had been kidnapped by Charlie and were forced to join its ranks. All day, our detachment would interrogate every adult male in what was called a County Fair. When not interrogating, members of the detachment processed captured enemy documents, weapons and enemy realia. A couple of times our unit was sent to undress dead enemy soldiers to forward their uniforms to Saigon.

There was a certain pattern to the interrogation of the Vietcong that were caught in fire fights. An infantry soldier or guard would bring the enemy soldier to the interrogation tent, often blindfolded and with an ID tag hanging from his neck. First we would question the guard. What was the prisoner doing when he was captured? Where and when was he captured? What was his attitude? Was he cocky, timid, talkative, helpful,? etc. Normally, infantry grunts were never that well informed. They were usually rough with the prisoner and that put the interrogators at a disadvantage. After the interrogator exhausted a checklist with all possible questions, he would prepare a report using a portable typewriter. That report would accompany the prisoner to higher headquarters for strategic interrogation.

For an entire year we performed endless interrogations, filled thousands of sandbags for shelters, dug holes for protection, became experts in putting up and disassembling tents, and watched the sick and dead being evacuated. The oddest interrogation took place inside of a field hospital, while the prisoner was sedated and his arm was being amputated.

Near the end of my tour, in July 1967, I received rotation orders assigning me back to the continental United States. That day, under a prisoner's tent in the Central Highlands, shirtless and sweaty after a long day of interrogation, I found out that I was going back to DLI. My orders read in part: "... report to Company B, Defense Language Institute, West Coast Branch, for training in the Polish language.

The Polish department was then located in building 274, on the north side of Soldier's Field. Its chairperson was Dr. Stefan Kaminski. Among its instructors were Messrs. Haska, Truskolaski, Wolfe, Palucki, Radzivill, Shumelda, Bevensee, and Kasparek-Obst. Also, my homeroom teacher and only female in the department, Mrs. Gabrielle Lubomirski, was part of the faculty.

In 1968 I left the Army, moved to San Jose, Calif. And subsequently took advantage of the GI Bill by obtaining degrees in psychology, computer science, Spanish literature, and curriculum and instruction.

In 1972, DLI hired me as a Spanish course writer, from where I moved to the Spanish department as instructor and supervisor. In 1976, my career took swiftly, when I moved to the Instructional Technology Division, Faculty Development Division and became course development coordinator for the Asian and Middle East languages. In 1981, I served as project manager for the DLI provost, from where I moved to the Curriculum Division, and then as Department Chair, Middle East course development department. Last and most importantly for my career, I served as dean of all the major DLI schools. In the following order, I supervised the Asian, Korean, Middle East, Slavic, and Romance languages.

What did I learn in the Army? What did I learn in Vietnam? What did I learn at DLI?

First of all, in the Army I learned discipline. The Army turned the amateur that I was into a professional. *An amateur does what he or she likes to do* and that's what I did before I joined the Army. Then, the Army forced me to do many things I did not want to do. First, I fought it, but when I knew I had no other alternative, I forced myself to enjoy whatever I was doing. Now, after an initial dislike, *I enjoy everything I do, which is the mark of a true professional.* Of course, I stay away from illegal or improper activities.

In Vietnam I learned to appreciate many things I took for granted before. I thank God every day that I can take a hot shower, that I can drink a cold beer, read without interruption, and no matter how onerous my job may become, it causes me little stress.

In Vietnam I also learned that one can get high without drugs, by doing repetitive activities that took me away from the stark reality to daydreaming. Filling sand bags was one of those activities. Now, I find therapy in walking alone, and playing with computers.

In Vietnam I also learned that only in the presence of serious conflict you can find the true nature of some people. In a war zone, individuals who look strong turn out to be weak and some who look weak act with courage. Now, long after Vietnam, I realize that I have to observe people under conflict before they can show me who they are. Life is the presence of conflicts and I welcome them. *Only dead people have no problems.*

After I became a Dean, one of the department chairs confided that I was the only person he knew who looked happy in the presence of problems and conflicts.

As a DLI student, I became the best in my French and Polish courses. In the middle of the course I was better than the students who were graduating. The secret I learned and I don't know how is contained in three A's, which I now give our new students in their orientation. It is called the Ben De La Selva triple "A" way to learn anything and it is contained in the words: *Attendance, Attention, and Application.* That is, *come to class every day, pay attention in class, and apply pluck and hard work.*

At DLI I learned how to understand people of all cultures. Early in my civilian career I noticed that people of different nationalities and cultures were only different at the surface (formal) level. Deep down (at the informal level) they were all the same. With that knowledge I tried to remove formality from all interchanges, and the real human being came up to meet me. I also learned that awards are only meaningful rewards in the eyes of the beholder, and not make the giver feel good. In short, the Army, Vietnam, and DLI gave me the formula for success.

However I would be remiss if I fail to mention that regardless of my mental and physical efforts, I would not be who I am today, and would not have the job I have, without the United States of America. Besides the gains I mentioned, I took advantage of the GI bill to get an education.

What I have offered is a glimpse of a one man's success story. Only in America, *a man from the jungle* can have the opportunity to succeed and become a dean in the best language school in the world. Only in America. ❖

Mrs. Sylvia Panetta helps Col. David McNerney cut a special cake for the opening of a new General Instructional facility

EVOLUTION
The McNerney Years (1981-1985)
A time to build at DLIFLC

With input from Col. (U.S.A., ret) David A. McNerney
DLIAA Newsletter XII - October 2006

Col. David A. McNerney was commandant of the Defense Language Institute Foreign Language Center (DLIFLC) from 1981 to 1985. He came to DLIFLC from the Training and Doctrine Command Operation Center (TRADOC) headquarters and was acutely aware of a number of major issues affecting DLIFLC. He also had a solid background in military construction, budget, manpower and civilian personnel management. He was specifically aware that DLIFLC was projected to double its student population within the coming five years. Recognizing that DLIFLC possessed an abundance of dedicated talent in the staff and faculty who only needed leadership and guidance, McNerney embarked on an ambitious and comprehensive program to enhance DLIFLC. McNerney retired 21 years ago, but every area described below had such a tremendous impact on language training and linguist management that the legacy still permeates the very fabric of DLIFLC's organization.

The construction program initiated and carried out by McNerney produced a wave of new construction activity that changed the face of the Presidio as no other building program has achieved before or since. His construction plan made a reality the Russian Village Complex at the southwestern tip of the Presidio; Munakata and Nicholson General Instruction Facilities; the Taylor Hall Personnel Processing Center; Collins Hall; Aiso Library; Belas Dining Facility; Hobson Student Activity Center; the Logistics Building; the Post Exchange; Price Fitness Center, and thirteen new dormitory buildings housing 1,350 students in two person rooms with private baths. This flurry of construction represented the largest building effort in Monterey County in the preceding 20 years. With sheer determination and an uncanny ability to get things done, McNerney was able to get $100 million of Title IV Department of Defense (DoD) construction money and receive approval for an expedited construction program.

In 1985, Colonel McNerney (far right) joins Craig Wilson (far left) and others in breaking ground for the future Nicholson Hall (Building 848)

Troop command reorganization. McNerney realized immediately that Troop Command was not organized in accordance with the U.S. Army training policy nor was it supportive of the language learning process at DLIFLC. It consisted of three 700 person companies (Headquarters, A and C) and was staffed with non-linguist leaders. He had the Adjutant General Branch commander replaced with a Military Intelligence officer and proceeded to replace all Platoon Sergeant and 1st Sergeant positions with language specific leaders so they could mentor their students throughout the learning process. He then reduced the company size to approximately 200 to 300 students and tied them closely to the school organization, activating Companies B, D and F. He also placed all officer and senior non-commissioned officer students in Company E, for better management, since they would have different processing and physical fitness standards than incoming soldiers with minimal military service.

The San Francisco Annex. A DLIFLC annex was established in the old Merchant Marine hospital on the grounds of the Presidio of San Francisco to handle the student population increase until the new classrooms were built in Monterey. The Presidio Annex, as it became known, consisted of approximately 600 Army students in German, Korean, and Spanish, organized as Companies G and H.

Military professional development. McNerney worked closely with DLIFLC's civilian union leadership to clear the way for military linguists to work side-by-side with civilian faculty in DLIFLC classrooms and converted all the previous Foreign Language Training Non Commissioned Officer/Petty Officer (NCO/PO) positions into a new position called Military Language Instructor (MLI), to give these personnel active teaching experience. This program created a very strong demand for assignment to DLIFLC by linguist NCOs/POs, since they recog-nized the significant career enhancement opportunity afforded by this assignment. It also ensured that DLIFLC would have the highest quality linguists returning to the Presidio of Monterey. McNerney insisted on establishing a comprehensive development program for all NCOs and POs assigned to the language school staff and faculty. All incoming linguists were immediately assigned as students to an accelerated or advanced language program to refresh and enhance their language skills. Over the course of their DLIFLC tour, they were rotated into Platoon Sergeant positions, in the companies, MLI positions in the language schools, and/or Subject Matter Expert (SME) duties on course development projects. This ensured that they were well-rounded professionally in both the military and linguistic skill components of their military occupational specialty.

Military linguist pay. McNerney had his staff prepare a proposed plan for military linguist pay. The final proposal consisted of a matrix showing language proficiency on one axis and the language difficulty categories on the other. This proposal was later enacted into law by Congress for all Department of Defense (DoD) military personnel.

Academic initiatives. Finding DLIFLC's instructional staff lumped into three unwieldy language groups, each headed by a "Group Chief," McNerney was able to get approval to reorganize into seven smaller language "schools" each under a "Director," which later on became "Dean." He was also able to get TRADOC approval to change the manpower staffing level from 1.52 instructors per student section to 1.85 instructors per student section. He revitalized the faculty development program for newer instructors and entered into an agreement with the Monterey Institute of International Studies for a Master's Degree in the Teaching of Foreign Languages for faculty members, using staff and faculty training funds for tuition. He proposed and got approval to increase the length of Arabic courses to 63 weeks, overcoming strong objections from the Air Force and Navy. He also proposed that the other Category IV languages (Chinese, Japanese and Korean) be extended to 63 weeks on a number of occasions, but did not receive approval during his tenure. In an effort to update language training materials both at DLIFLC and around the globe, he secured funding for more modern technology and equipment, including: large antennae to receive live foreign language broadcasts via satellite; video cassette recorders that could play the European speed of PAL I, PAL II and SECAM in addition to the U.S. NTSC standard to give students the capability to view recent video tapes from a wide range of countries (including those behind the Iron Curtain); and video teleconferencing equipment to conduct refresher training throughout the world using DLIFLC instructors. He also insisted on a high level of cultural awareness in the language learning process and procured a wide range of ethnic musical instruments, a number of pianos and even a Chinese Dragon for use during cultural events.

Language course development. Responsibility for the development of major language courses and non-resident instructional material was vested in a single directorate and was a disaster in terms of organization and staff. He assembled four separate proposals for word processors and was able to get a reluctant TRADOC to approve them although they wanted a single standard. The procurement of a Japanese-English machine serves as an example of some of the difficulties of this endeavor. After the head of the Japanese Department found a suitable machine in Japan, there were a myriad of procurement problems. The machine was a Fujitsu, but it was a model not sold in the United States. Fujitsu agreed to sell two machines and provide special arrangements for maintenance – probably as a matter of national honor. When the machines finally arrived all the instructions and even the bill of landing were in Japanese. The first non-Roman alphabet machine to arrive was an Arabic word processor with dual print wheels for Arabic and English that had been developed for the Saudis. The TRADOC Word Processing Officer later admitted to never having seen such a machine. Cyrillic alphabet machines also significantly improved the pace of course development work in Russian and other East European languages. Initial Chinese and Korean word processors did not have an English capability and for a while Chinese and Korean clerks had to cut and paste the material, but even this was a significant improvement. In addition to basic course development, progress was made in developing new *Headstart* programs and for some existing programs, a video track was developed under contract with UCLA using their studios with technical direction by a DLIFLC department head. There was tremendous progress made in non-resident training materials including Forces Command Language Maintenance Refresher and Improvement Course (FLAMRIC) and various other language refresher and maintenance programs.

Testing. When McNerney arrived at DLIFLC testing was also an unmitigated disaster with poorly written Defense Language Proficiency Tests (DLPT) I and II, and proficiency levels that did not track with other language agencies or academic standards. Most DLPTs were published in only one version, so linguists could virtually memorize the test items over the years. Since the tests did not evaluate speaking ability, the results provided no real index of a linguist's fluency in the foreign language. With the expertise of Dr. Ray Clifford (DLIFLC provost, then chancellor), McNerney instituted a completely new generation of DLPTs. A General Officers Steering Committee (GOSC) mandated DLPT III was created in multiple versions using the Interagency Roundtable Language (ILR) proficiency standards. DLPT III first had a taped speaking test; then it was changed to an Oral Proficiency Interview. At that time cryptologic linguists did not have to take the DLPT. Course grades determined graduation status. McNerney persuaded the National Security Agency to support giving all students the DLPT to ensure that the test was taken seriously, in line with GOSC emphasis. As a stopgap measure, they supported recalibrating the older DLPTs so that scores lined up with other agencies. McNerney gave great visibility to testing. He had every visitor briefed on the new test and emphasized the importance of standards. As DLPT III was being developed, a DLPT IV was being planned. All of this required a tremendous long-term effort.

Civilian Personnel. McNerney found himself with a civilian workforce, one third of which were on temporary status, some for very extended periods of time. Since temporary hires did not get step pay increases, this was a serious morale issue. Over time he was able to double the size of the faculty and reduce the temporary hires to less than five percent. He also insisted on a robust use of performance pay which had been previously neglected. A major issue was that the faculty was divided into General Service and Excepted Service categories severely hindering personnel reassignments. He was able to get Department of the Army approval to reclassify all academic positions into Excepted Service. Then, with the assistance of Ms. Virginia Lamb, a GS-13 personnel management specialist, he started working on a concept which eventually would award faculty pay based on academic education, experience and performance rather than tenure. Officially initiated by the next Commandant, Col. Monte Bullard, this concept became the Faculty Personnel System and was finally approved by Congress some fifteen years later.

Teachers Union. When McNerney arrived at DLIFLC the federal employee Union had had a long standing adversarial relationship with the Command Group. This was resolved over time with the removal of a series of minor disagreements and a new Union contract that was perceived as fair by both sides. The relationship significantly improved with the election of Mr. Alfie Khalil as Union President after McNerney tenure, leading to a very productive long-term relationship.

Administrative support. Major improvements were made in logistic support with the conversion to an automated Property Book and inventory system. Additionally, construction of the new Logistics Center with a concrete floor permitted workers to use a fork lift to handle pallets of books rather than the hand cart. Word processors were introduced to expedite secretarial work and paper shredders were introduced to destroy old student tests. A major long-term effort to replace DLIFLC's mainframe Harris computer, which required an inordinate programming effort, with an IBM computer, was also accomplished.

Staff meetings and quarterly award presentations. To keep communications constantly flowing, McNerney had a staff meeting every Tuesday, including his headquarters staff, the school directors (later deans), staff offices, military units, and the garrison support personnel. Additionally, his quarterly awards presentations ensured anyone receiving any award at any level during the quarter, received it from the commandant. This included major cash awards like Sustained Superior Performance or Special Acts, but also length of service awards and even flag presentations for new citizens. The individuals, their friends, and the supervisors were invited, ensuring a large audience for all the honorees.

Teamwork and cooperation. McNerney was able to achieve an unprecedented level of teamwork, cohesiveness and camaraderie among the faculty and staff. He jump-started this evolution towards better communication by use of a weekly social gathering that he dubbed "Commandant's Call." On Wednesdays after class was over, the faculty and staff would gather at the Officers Club at 3:45 p.m.

and spend the rest of the duty day socializing with supervisors, peers and subordinates. People who did not see each other for weeks or even months because of busy schedules had a chance to talk business or pleasure for an hour or so. Anyone could approach McNerney, the provost or the senior staff and engage them in conversations that encompassed a wide range of topics. They would talk about the budget, academic matters, course development, testing, the non-resident program, the Union, and all sorts of problems, issues and challenges. McNerney, particularly, listened carefully – even took notes and made sure follow-up action was taken where appropriate. These sessions generated an enormous amount of good will and cohesiveness not seen before or after the McNerney era. He also sent an individual personalized note to each staff and faculty member on their birthdays thanking them for their hard work at DLIFLC. Both he and Mrs. McNerney made a point of knowing each and every faculty member by name (along with pertinent family information). The resulting atmosphere was upbeat, collegial, almost resembling the interpersonal relations of a huge extended family, and fostered a "can-do" attitude. McNerney did not ensconce himself in the headquarters building, but was constantly on the move dropping in on classes, faculty, and staff in their work environment. He was totally, completely and personally in touch with everyone and everything that was going on at DLIFLC. In sum, McNerney's tenure brought about a wide range of significant improvements to DLIFLC during a period of major increase in the student population and associated faculty expansion. His accomplishments in the areas described above are forever impressed in the minds of many DLIFLC faculty and staff, who will always remember with nostalgia "The McNerney Years". ❖

Col. Monte Bullard (right) assumes command in August 1985

The evolution of team teaching at DLI - 1985 to 2005 –
DLI *GLOBE* - April 2005
With input from Col. Monte Bullard, U.S. Army (ret)

Two of the fundamental changes that resulted in the transformation of the Defense Language Institute from a good to a great organization were the introduction of Team Teaching and the change from the Civil Service GS system to the Faculty Personnel System or FPS. This article will address both, but mainly the former.

The early beginnings of Team Teaching at the Defense Language Institute could be first gleaned in early 1985 from correspondence between Colonel Monte Bullard, then the U.S. Army Attaché in Hong Kong, and Major Robert Hunt, Asian School Training Officer (now called Associate Dean). Bullard had been a Chinese student at DLI in 1959 and had spent much of his Army career as a Chinese Foreign Area Officer. At the time, Hunt maintained that the idea of a six-instructor teaching team came to Bullard when the latter first observed that while western students in Beijing were housed two to a room, six Chinese students occupied the same size room and got along fairly well. While Hunt's version of this "AHA!" experience could be contested, the truth is that Bullard thought a six-instructor team was ideal to work harmoniously and independently with three sections of students (at the same level), taking care of absences without borrowing teachers from other groups. Bullard's idea of Team Teaching was driven by two of his real intended purposes, to flatten the supervisory chain and to inject responsibility and accountability into the system. He thought one of the big problems at DLI was the too many layers of civilian supervision, four to be exact: Provost (GS15), deans (GS13), chairs (GS12), and supervisors (GS11). At the end, he decided to convert the GS11 permanent "supervisors" into GS11 "team mentors." He also created temporary GS11 team mentor positions for new applicants. The length of the temporary appointment was linked to the duration of the class the team was assigned to teach. These new leaders would lack supervisory authority, but could take care of business by persuading and convincing rather than by using precious time to enforce minor rules and barking orders. With a mentor in every team, Bullard in effect was pushing accountability and decision making to the level of the teachers, one of his principal ideas.

Note: All promotions to GS11 permanent supervisory positions were halted. These positions had been allocated at the ratio of one per fifteen instructors. The new temporary non-supervisory positions were allocated at a ratio of one per six instructors.

Bullard recalls that although he got some good ideas from Hunt before arriving at DLI, his real "AHA" experience was realized when he visited a certain language department on input day. He found that not only did the teachers not know which class they would teach that day; they had done no preparation and had no real idea of who their students would be. That surprise, combined with Bullard's reading of the management book "In Search of Excellence" by Tom Peters, gave him some ideas on what to do during his DLI watch. He also noted that teachers were not being treated very well, in that the maximum pay they could receive and remain in the classroom was that of a GS-09, at the time only around $23,000 a year. Promotions, he thought, had to be allowed for quality teaching, not for longevity, as in the Civil Service system. He knew that after reaching the grade of GS-09, teachers could not get promoted (and stay in the classroom), and couldn't be fired either. To be promoted, teachers had to leave the classroom and be supervisors. He also found that many of the instructors had never had any significant training in language teaching. Teachers knew their language well, but had no idea about testing theory, etc. In Bullard's words "We had to find a way to allow and support teachers to get advanced language teaching degrees and participate in professional language teaching organizations and activities. They were the best, but they didn't write much in the professional journals."

The key idea about Team Teaching though was to improve the teachers' incentive and to increase their accountability for the student's learning. It was important that the same teachers follow the same students throughout the course and that the teachers be judged on the outcomes reached by the students, and not just by the number of students who graduated.

When asked how the idea of 6 teachers per team came about, Bullard said that the actual numbers came when he was driving across Texas with Dr. Ray Clifford (then DLI Academic Dean). He drove and Clifford took notes. On the road they designed the 6 person 2 teacher-per-section team that later had to be revised a bit to accommodate teams of four sections. However, in his resolve to have three-section teams, Bullard directed the scheduling division to arrange for three-section inputs. Thus, with exception of small mention at that time. For example, he wanted to republish DLI's language programs, inputs arrived in multiples of three sections for many years.

As conveyed to Hunt, several of Bullard's ideas prior to his arrival as DLI Commandant, sound very radical today, not to wiring diagram so that it looked like an inverted pyramid, with the school, departments, and teams on top of the diagram, and the Commandant at the bottom. His thinking stemmed from the belief that "we had to make all of the staff and faculty view themselves as supporting the teachers, not controlling them".

Before Bullard's arrival in August 1985, instructors were generally assigned to supervisors, who took care of one, two, three, and sometimes four classes (each composed of several sections), and supervised 10, 20, or 30 teachers. The supervisor was in charge of teachers who taught classes at different levels and although most instructors stayed with the same group of students throughout the course, it was not uncommon for an instructor to be pulled out of one group to cover absences in another group, and then end up teaching students who might be in the beginning, in the middle, and at the end of the course. Furthermore, the supervisor's classes could be scattered in different areas of the same floor, or on different floors, or even in different buildings. Many times instructors teaching the same students were located far from each other, making coordination of instruction very difficult. Until 1993, for example, all Arabic teachers were located on the second floor of Pomerene Hall, while students had classes in the first and third floors. There were also Arabic classes in Nisei Hall and Munakata Hall, making some of the teachers walk from building to building.

Having been a Chinese student, Bullard was familiar with the Chinese program and knew several of the instructors from his days at DLI and from Taiwan. Therefore, he was interested in organizing the first teams in the Asian School. One day he called the Asian School Dean (me) into his office, and bypassing the Provost, directed the former to start a team in the Chinese department. Bullard's ideas of Team Teaching included complete team independence from most established DLI practices. The team would plan its own curriculum, write its own class and teachers' schedules, and decide whether or not to use the formally-tried and traditional audio-lingual materials available to everyone. Although still legally under a supervisor, the team was loosely managed by someone appointed as team leader, or mentor. In retrospect, Team Teaching "a la Bullard" was flexible enough to coexist with any and all language teaching approaches used at DLI since the mid- 1980s. Bullard's radical plan stood the Institute on its head. The first casualty was lock step instruction; another sacred cow was the faculty to section ratio that eventually changed from 1.33 to 2 instructors per 10-student section. Then, one by one the permanent supervisors were replaced by temporary GS-11 non-supervisory mentors, and eventually by team leaders. Furthermore, Bullard was in effect the supervisor of the first teams, in that he would tell the team members directly what to do, to the dismay of the chairs and supervisors. When Bullard left DLI in October 1987 there were well functioning teams springing up in every school, the most successful being in the East European School (Czech department), under the leadership of Jawdat Yonan.

Another notion in Bullard's scheme included the use of computers. According to Bullard, it was time to move into the computer world for publishing. Many teachers and students complained about the cookie cutter textbooks. His thought was to produce a textbook on a computer that could easily be revised by the teaching team. The teachers would have complete authority to change the book anyway they liked, but they would be judged at the end on how their students did on the Defense Language Proficiency Test, DLPT. In theory each team could teach from different teaching materials. Another related idea was for the teaching teams to think about and prepare computer assisted exercises and support programs. Some Czech department teachers led the way at the time and provided excellent examples of what was possible in tech learning. Bullard used some of these Czech teachers to brief the Pentagon brass and their enthusiasm was key to selling the Team Teaching program.

However, before implementing any drastic changes, Bullard knew he had to deal with the local Union. Accordingly, in early 1986 he organized a deans' (then called directors) offsite and invited Union president Natalie Fryberger to hear his innovative ideas for the first time. In the fall of 1986 Bullard involved Fryberger and the Union Board in negotiating a Team Teaching policy, a document that was signed by Dr. Clifford (then Provost) in January 1987. With the signing of this official document other actions were initiated, the most important one being formal Team Building training, which required every newly formed team to go thru a week's workshop organized by the Faculty and Staff Development Division. The document was further revised in March 2003.

Bullard also began what was then called the "New Personnel System," or NPS, that would organize the Institute like a civilian university, with professional ranks and titles, and away from constraining civil service regulations. The NPS idea was forcefully pushed forward from year to year by Dr. Ray Clifford over the initial opposition of several commandants. The initiative finally became a reality in 1997/1998 as the "Faculty Personnel System" or FPS. In retrospect, Team Teaching and the FPS began radical changes that in their maturity transformed DLI from a good institution into a great institution. No other changes, either before or after, have made such a great impact.

Part of the rationale for the FPS was that the Training and Doctrine Command, DLI's parent organization, was evaluating DLI with the same measures that Fort Benning used in their training programs. Obviously, that didn't fit. What DLI was teaching was broader and fit more into the notion of education versus training. DLI also had to find a way to get teachers promoted and still remain in the classroom, but civil service regulations didn't permit that. Overall what Bullard wanted was a system that allowed good teachers, based on education and creativity in teaching, to get promoted and stay in the classroom. Eventually, DLI would build in a period where teachers could opt in or out of the new system so those who were content with drawing low pay and working hard could still remain with us, even in the old system. However, Bullard believed the vast majority would strive to improve themselves in the field of language teaching and that in turn would have an impact on the language ability of the graduates.

Bullard was succeeded as Commandant by Col. Todd Poch (Oct87-Sep88) and Col. Ronald Cowger (Sep88-Aug89), who made no significant changes to Team Teaching. However, the next commandant, Col. Donald Fischer (Aug89-Jan93), introduced several changes. One of them was authorizing one GS11 permanent team mentor position per team. Some teams had already a former supervisor occupying that position. However, in teams with only temporary team mentors, the incumbent had an opportunity to attain tenure. Later, Fischer determined that one mentor per team was insufficient to adequately perform all the duties in their job description. Therefore, the mentor position was divided into two team coordinator positions with many shared duties and a general division in emphasis between academic and administrative responsibilities. These new team coordinator positions were labeled Teaching and Program Coordinator; and shared a common job description with optional break-out duties. Both positions were temporary NTE one year, with renewable appointments linked to the duration of assigned classes.

Another change instituted by Fischer was the introduction of the Learner Focused Instructional Day (LFID), which emphasized student centered instruction, established the idea of split sections to enhance speaking, and initiated the 7th hour of instruction. This last idea was later discarded, as one more daily hour of instruction did not to produce a more proficient student. At that time many of the split sections were still conducted in teachers' offices. In the personnel area, Fischer went further and pushed for a second GS-11 (now called coordinator) per team. During Col. Vladimir Sobichevsky's tenure (Jan93-Dec95), an idea sprang in the Germanic School, under the leadership of Dr. Neil Granoien. The brainchild of Sabine Atwell and Gordana Stanchfield, both German chairs, this idea was first called the "Condo" concept, which was to collocate all teachers and students together geographically, as opposed to being scattered all over as in the past. Dr. Granoien implemented the idea in his school swiftly and over the objections of most faculty. Later on, however, when schools or departments had to change locations, it was a logical step to fall into the "Condo" scheme.

Fischer's policy of split sections and the pressure to further increase proficiency led to the need for extra rooms for those split sections. During those years the Consolidated Team Concept (CTC) was born. CTC included two elements; the first one was that the teachers and students must be geographically close to each other; the second that there would be enough rooms to conduct at least two split sessions per section per day (total of 6). Thus the formula was created that every three-section team should have three classrooms, one breakout room, and two or three other rooms for teachers' offices.

With the official introduction of the FPS in late 1997, teams' dynamics changed. To become a team leader it was no longer necessary to get promoted from GS-09 to GS-11. Team leaders could be selected competitively or be appointed by the school dean. Although most GS-11s continued performing the team leaders' job after converting to the FPS, little by little individuals in the professorial ranks took over the team leader positions.

During the tenures of Col. Daniel Devlin (Feb96-Dec00) and Col. Kevin Rice (Dec00-Jun03), Team Teaching was left practically undisturbed. Two years ago, however, during Col. Michael Simone's watch (2003-Present) the Team Teaching policy was slightly revised, and emphasis was placed again on Team Teaching training.

In 2004, the demands to produce better students caused DLI to assure the users higher proficiency rates in exchange for smaller sections, students with higher DLAB score, and longer courses. Of those three, the services agreed to only the first one, smaller sections. Thus, in various languages, inputs are now arriving with fewer than 10 students per section, i.e., 8 in Spanish and French, 6 in Russian. This latest initiative has been named the Proficiency Enhancement Program, or PEP.

The pressure to produce higher proficiency results and the need for more space due to the increase in student input have cause the DLI leadership to pause and rethink the Team Teaching and CTC concepts. Fortunately, wisdom has prevailed and no noteworthy changes have been introduced. In summary, Team Teaching basically remains the way Col. Monte Bullard envisioned it and implemented it.

Although in this article we claim that Team Teach improved DLI in many aspects, it will be difficult to back up that claim without statistics. The following chart uses 1985/86 as the baseline for measuring the improvement in the percentage of students reaching the 2/2/1+ levels (light gray), and 2+/2+/2 (dark gray). In the first ten years after the implementation of Team Teaching we see a threefold increase in 2/2/1+ and almost a fivefold increase in 2+/2+/2.

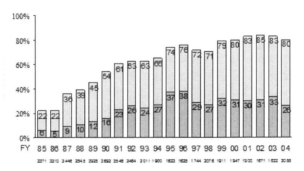

Proficiency improvements from 1985-86 to 2004 in terms of levels 2/2/1+ (light gray) and 2+/2+/2 (dark gray)

❖

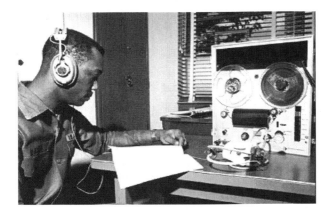

Soldier using a 40-pound reel-to-reel tape recorded to do his homework in the barracks

Evolution of technology in the classroom – from the 1940s to the present

DLIAA Newsletter XII – October 2006

There was nothing high-tech about the early days at the Army Language School, as the Defense Language Institute Foreign Language Center (DLIFLC) was known back in the late 1940s, and students and teachers alike used orange crates for desks. Obtaining blackboards was a major step forward at the time, and teachers had to make do with simple textbooks and the projection of their own voices to teach students languages.

During the 1950, teachers produced textbooks with manual typewriters and in some languages the characters had to be manually written down with a pen or brushes. Audio-visual aids were exploited to a great extent. Apart from a wealth of pictorial aids, a wide range of three dimensional objects were utilized, as well as mock-ups of battle sites known as military terrain (or sand) tables. A push to introduce 78 RPM records in the late 40's and early 50's did not last long, as these could only be played in class and were not durable enough to be shuffled from classroom to classroom. In very few classes, students were issued record players and records for homework practice, but only during the initial pronunciation phase of the program. As for 78 RPM record labs, there is no written record available, and only scanty recollection from either students or teachers of that era.

It was not until the 1950s that the reel-to-reel tape recorder was introduced. This large 40-pound monster was used by the teacher in the classroom, where the same dialogues and mechanical drills contained in the textbooks were played over and over while the students repeated, substituted, modified, transformed, and expanded the models provided on the tapes. In some buildings a contraption between a classroom and a lab (called CLAB) was assembled. This contrivance consisted of a strip built around the classroom walls where a tape recorder and 10 student headsets could be plugged in. This setup was mainly used to administer tests to groups of students without going to a lab. The reel-to-reel system was later converted into 36-position labs, where now three sections of students could be made to perform more of the same drills in unison, with only one teacher at the console. Obviously, the ratio of teachers needed for each section of 10 students was reduced to a minimum of 1:33. Later on, students could take the bulky tape recorder to their barracks or home, and perform the same drills in a more individualized fashion. They could memorize the daily dialogue, which had been dissected into segments so as to provide a progressive lengthening of words into phrases, then into sentences, and finally into full dialogue lines. As dialogues were normally between two individuals, the student, with the help of the recordings, would memorize both dialogue parts and the following day pair up with another student to recite the lines in front of the teacher in class. As Voice of America recordings were received, they were duplicated and the tapes issued to students.

Authentic reading materials consisted of newspapers and magazines that the language departments obtained several months after their publication. In the 1950s, some of the labs, auditoriums, and the bigger classrooms were used to show 16mm films that contained training materials and sometimes old movies. In the late 1960s, the overhead projector was introduced. The teacher was now able to use a piece of acetate and draw verb and other charts that he or she could project onto a screen. Later on these teacher-made charts could be duplicated and used by other teachers. Eventually, each teacher was issued a set of transparencies that were developed with each new course. In the early 1970s, some teachers made use of circular carrousels attached to a projector containing 35mm slides that projected onto a screen. The same principle was used with filmstrip kits, which advanced the slides in synchronization with a cassette tape player.

The cassette player was the big technological leap in the early and mid-1970s. The use of cassettes allowed students for the first time to carry their players from the classroom to the barracks and do some of the listening exercises on an individual basis. The first cassette players were about the size of a cereal box, and weighed several pounds. They were capable of recording, which some instructors took advantage of by assigning speaking tasks as homework, or recorded mock oral proficiency tests for the students. In the 1970s and 1980s, the cassette lab replaced the reel-to-reel lab, with a recorder installed in each student station. At this time, being able to play tapes at their own pace, students could do transcription and gisting (summarizing) exercises in the lab. During these two decades, the videocassette recorder (VCR) was introduced. Not only were teachers able to play cultural programs that the language departments purchased for the program, but also movies were eventually available. The ability to make their own videos at the Institute studios set off the creative juices of the faculty, who produced and modernized lots of adjunct materials to supplement old and new language courses.

For a short time in the late 1980s, the Institute experimented with wireless labs. In each building, certain classrooms were equipped with thin wire-antennas attached to the walls near the ceiling. Each classroom was also equipped with a rolling big box containing a cassette player with listening materials. The box sent signals to the wires, which in turn send the same signals to the students' headsets. Accordingly, students could move around the classroom with their wireless headsets on. Reception problems plagued these devices, with resultant failure.

The stand-alone PC computer, without a hard disk, appeared on the scene in the late 1980s. These were first used in conjunction with laser-disc players. For example, in 1988 DLIFLC obtained permission to convert the Arabic commercial program "From the Gulf to the Ocean" from film strip/cassette to laser disc technology. In this program, a laser disc player hooked up to a computer was used to deliver the introduction of Arabic lessons in 1990. The Arabic program was thus the first program at DLIFLC to have a stand-alone computer in every classroom. In the early 1990s, there was an attempt to introduce the use of Apple computers at the Institute level. Accordingly, a short training course was mandatory for all instructors. As there was a dearth of software programs in the Apple platform, the IBM PC was the preferred option. Because Arabic course developers had been working on computer-based exercises for a couple of years, in 1990 the first stand-alone computer lab was established in the Middle East School, then only one school. These standalone computer labs were established in all DLIFLC schools and most used commercial software and DLIFLC developed programs. Unfortunately, many of these programs contained countless fill-in, multiple choice, and mechanical exercises. At the beginning these labs were not networked, providing only materials contained in each computer's hard drive, on diskettes, or CDs, many of them developed in house. However, throughout the late 1990s, several schools were able to establish networked computer labs. For example, in 1997 two computer labs were networked in Middle East Schools I and II. Other DLIFLC schools subsequently networked their labs, using commercial software and DLIFLC-developed programs, and included Internet access. By this time, the Educational Technology Division was producing language materials on CDs, and the language departments were able to have CD libraries available for students in the lab and to loan for home use, as more and more students were purchasing desktop computers for their own use. In the meantime, students were still carrying cassette players back and forth to the barracks, but these players were now made the size of a Walkman and besides recording capabilities, some of them could adjust the speed of recording without altering the pitch. In 1998, in a trial attempt to supplement the then recently developed Spanish course, every student in one Spanish class was issued a laptop computer. Laptops were principally used for assigning homework, which consisted of a CD that included some of the same workbook exercises in the textbooks. The program was discontinued mainly because the laptops were damaged beyond repair after just 24 weeks. Several laptops needed hard-drives and floppy drives replaced or repaired; latches were broken, buttons not working, etc. Unfortunately, the warranties had expired, and, alas, repairs could not be made. In 2000-2001, after many DLIFLC buildings had been networked, a program dubbed TEC-1 began in the European and Latin American School (ELA). It consisted of a rolling cart equipped with a computer and 32-inch monitor, a VCR, and DVD player. This was the first Institute-level attempt to network a classroom computer to other computers in the building and to the Internet.

In 2001, an Institute initiative made ELA the recipient of two Multi-Media Labs (MML), installed on the third floor of Munakata Hall (Bldg 610), which were connected to the DLIFLC-wide network. These labs brought colorful text, audio, and video from the teacher's console to individual student computer stations. In these 33-station labs, instructors had the ability to launch individual text, audio, and video files and send them to students for self-paced work. Instructors were able to give students lots of practice with Performance Final Learning Objectives (FLOs). At this time, instructors began developing materials in their offices and delivered these materials through a central clearing office to the MMLs. Two other labs were constructed in the Korean and Russian schools. These labs contained some new features, such as down under monitors, an Elmo Camera, and a wireless microphone that allowed the teacher to talk to all the students through their earphones from any place in the room. The second generation of MMLs installed in the rest of the schools was of the Linguatronics/Genesis type, replacing the initial hardware and software assembled by the Tandberg (now Sanako) Language Lab Company. As with any modernization, the old and the new labs co-existed. Due to budgetary and other constraints, some of the schools could not install new labs and found it necessary to leave the old cassette labs in place. When the MMLs were first installed, there were no course materials ready for them, and the training offered by the lab company was not adequate for developing language materials.

Accordingly, the schools felt under pressure to immediately digitize all the audio and video materials contained in the old courses. Fortunately, the new labs could combine text, audio, and colorful video on the same screen and in fact increased students' motivation greatly. Digitizing course materials using PCs made it easy to go to the next step, which was the creation of CDs containing documents (.doc), audio (.mp3), and video (.avi) files. This technological advance made it possible to compress files in ways not imagined before. As a result, for example, the Spanish course homework numbering some 30 audiocassettes could all fit on one CD. Accordingly, each school started issuing MP3 players capable of playing CDs with text and audio files. Additionally, some departments purchased MP3 players with an internal storage capacity of 512 megabytes. With the introduction of MP3 players, some schools flatly discontinued using audio-cassette players and tapes in all their programs. But as with the labs, audiocassette and MP3 players were allowed to coexist. To the early experience with MMLs followed Classroom 21, also known as the "Blue Room", an effort funded by the Training and Doctrine Command (TRADOC) that consisted of a teacher console, 36 student-computer stations, plus two huge screens on the wall. As with MMLs, the teacher sent files that could be viewed in the stations as well as on the big screens. Classroom 21 had also video teleconferencing capability.

As early as 2002, with the creation of the Emerging Languages Task Force (ELTF), the use of tablet PCs and Smart Boards, or interactive white boards, was initiated. Accordingly, students were issued portable tablets for classroom and homework use. As most ELTF courses were being developed as they were taught, the course contents were immediately digitized and loaded onto a server. Students would then select the appropriate tasks assigned by the teachers and would download them to their PCs. The success of the interactive white boards in ELTF was so great that the Institute leadership decided to install them DLIFLC-wide. Through such a device all text, audio, and video materials could be delivered. The inter-activeness of the Smart Board has literally transformed the classroom into an interactive working and learning environment, with the combined power of a projector, computer and whiteboard. Teachers can do everything they do on their computer – and more, by simply using their index finger as a mouse, to touch the whiteboard and highlight key points, access applications and websites, and write notes in electronic ink. Instructors are then able to save their work to files that can be reused later, printed, e-mailed or posted to a website. At the end of 2004, there was a Smart Board in every DLIFLC classroom. In 2004, the Institute saw an opportunity to introduce in large scale the use of laptops. The ELTF programs had already switched the previous year from tablet PCs to laptops. In 2005, the other DLIFLC schools followed suit and started issuing laptops to every student. One of the assignments was to have students record speaking tasks that were sent to the teacher by e-mail. The teacher in turn would listen and review the file and gave feedback to the student in class. In 2005-06, iPods began making their way into DLIFLC classrooms. With a bigger display and much bigger storage capacity than MP3 players, students were better able to navigate through the myriad of exercises stored on the devices. The latest iPods could store 20 and more gigabytes of audio files, making it possible for students to carry a whole language course in a gadget the size of a pack of cigarettes. As advertised, these tiny giants could carry an entire library of music – up to 20,000 songs. Presently, some of the schools (e.g., the Middle East Schools) have set up websites on DLIFLC's intranet and have made available hundreds of hours of video programs and movies from the multi-language channel SCOLA, Aljazeera, and other sources. These files can in turn be converted to iPod-ready files for students to download into their pocket-size prodigies. As new generations of iPods are being purchased, the imagination of the teachers is finding other ways to utilize them to enhance language teaching and learning. True to the advertising slogan: *"Movies, TV shows and music are now playing on an iPod near you."*

Since the 1950s, advances in technology have been systematically applied to language teaching and learning at DLIFLC. Appropriately, DLIFLC has gradually moved from chalkboards and overhead projectors to Smart boards, from reel-to-reel labs to multi-media labs, and from analog tape recorders to digital iPods. Without doubt, one can say with confidence that the application of technology at DLIFLC has indeed come a long way.

❖

Evolution of administrative and course development technology
From the 1940s to the present
DLIAA Newsletter XII – October 2006

Parallel to the introduction of new technologies in the classroom were advances in the admin/course development area. In the 1960's manual typewriters were replaced by electric ones, some of them possessing internal memory. Language courses in the 1970s were developed using these electric typewriters. In the early 1980s, some DLI administrators started using dumb terminals connected to a mainframe computer to do word processing, and for the first time communicated by email using a primitive system call PROFS. In some course development projects, camera-ready copies were used for the text books, while audiocassettes and video tapes were created Institute wide at studios to complement the textbooks. Electric typewriters were replaced first by English-only word processors and later on by bilingual ones. Obviously, the romance languages were first in the acquisition of machines, ahead of Arabic and Korean. These new bilingual word processors were bought with a 3-foot high tower that could store 20 megabytes of materials. Japanese and Chinese had to wait until the 1990s, as the developers kept writing characters by hand (or brush) or, as in the case of Chinese, used a manual device with 7000 ideograms arranged upside down and backwards that looked more like a Da Vinci designed apparatus.

Eventually, DLI contracted with XEROX to provide the Institute with more modern word processors that could handle several foreign languages, and were able to process sophisticated layouts. In the 1980s, for the first time the stand alone Xerox word processor with Arabic fonts was introduced and distributed to each Arabic department. These machines had large screens and thanks to them course developers were able to redo and reprint Arabic text books that had lost their print quality over time. Subsequently, stand-alone computers made their way into main offices and CD teams. In 1993, telephone modems were installed in each office computer, but the email program used was the still primitive PROFS system. Soon thereafter Microsoft Outlook was introduced, facilitating the communication among administrators. As one by one all DLI buildings were wired and interconnected, each office, and then each instructor was issued a computer and an email address. Thereafter, course developers, as well as teachers, could develop course materials in diskettes and CDs, and could send those materials across DLI. In the last three decades, while some course development projects were formed to write resident courses, others developed materials for the field. Accordingly, throughout the years the field received tons of textbooks, cassette tapes, VCRs, and CDs. However, with the advent of computers and the internet, and the ability to store and send files thru cyberspace, programs were acquired to develop interactive materials on websites for field use. Some of these programs, however, could also benefit resident basic course students. One present example is the GLOSS program.

GLOSS (formerly DLI-Lang Net) provides easy access to online language materials. There are by now nearly 1500 lessons in 11 languages. These materials, based on authentic materials and loaded with useful feedback and cultural notes, are specifically developed to target many of the common trouble areas for language learners striving to enhance their proficiency and move from the plus level (1+, 2+, etc.) to the next full level as described by the Inter-Agency Language Roundtable scale. Graduates, as well as non-military language learners throughout the world, can connect to GLOSS by visiting its freely accessible materials at www.lingnet.org, where they are able to choose the appropriate language, proficiency level, topical domain, skill modality, competency, and resource type (text and audio) for their needs. Each lesson is a stand-alone unit, can be completed within one to two hours, and provides an experience similar to what a student would receive in a classroom situation. These lessons are being employed in a variety of ways in the later stages of instruction in several DLI basic course programs, as well.

As with technology applications in the classroom, offices and course development teams have kept pace with technological advances to support resident classroom teachers and teachers in the field. ❖

The Berlin Wall monument.
The Multi-Language School is in the background

THE BERLIN WALL MONUMENT
Berlin Wall finally arrives at DLI
DLIAA Newsletter VII - July 2005

"Pieces of the Berlin Wall first appeared at the Presidio of Monterey back in September 1992, when the International Language Culture Foundation (ILCF) obtained a wall fragment and unveiled it at an informal ceremony at the International Language and Culture Center (ILCC), now Weckerling Center. On that occasion, James Broz, ILCF board member, presented the piece to the then DLI Commandant Col. Donald C. Fischer, for his contributions and work at DLI and for helping the ILCF. The ILCF had been founded in 1987 by a handful of DLI academics to promote excellence in language studies worldwide." (The above excerpts were taken from a DLI *GLOBE* article published on Oct 29, 1992).

Furthermore, as recent as May of this year, the Institute acquired three complete sections of the Wall thanks to serendipity and the relentless efforts of Billy "Skip" Johnson, the current Installation

Inspector General. Many who have known Skip for years were amazed to know about his involvement because he never mentioned the historic episode, nor did he reveal how the three concrete slabs were obtained by DLI through him. If you have not seen these slabs, please visit the area between Nisei, Nakamura, and Pomerene Halls, otherwise known as the Language Day Quad. There, in contrast to the DLI structural design of the 50s, 60s, and 70s, stand three 12 feet concrete slabs that once separated East from West Berlin.

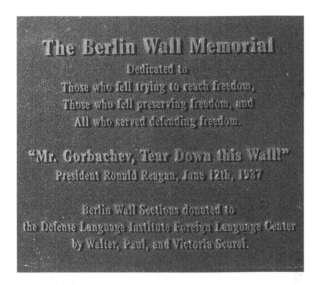

Plaque located at the base of the
Berlin Wall monument

The real story of Skip's involvement began one day in December 2001 when he went to visit his sister in Phoenix, Arizona. There he met one of her neighbors, Walter Scurei, then 69, who had grown up in East Berlin during the Soviet occupation of East Germany after WWII. In fact, Scurei was in East Berlin when the wall came down and at that time was able to secure several pounds of wall that he donated to relatives and friends.

During one of his several visits to Scurei's house in Phoenix, Skip became intrigued by three huge concrete blocks standing in the backyard. Not able to contain his curiosity, Skip sharply asked: "What's that?" Then Scurei, in a tale worthy of the One Thousand

and One Nights, explained to the astonished Skip how the slabs had gotten there.

On April 27th, 2002, Ami Wu, writing for the Monterey Herald briefly described the story as follows: "Scurei found the Berlin wall slabs at a nearby warehouse in 1998. They were abandoned by Arizona based hotel tycoon Irvin Dreyer III and Noel Heller, who purchased them for $110,000 in 1990 as an investment from former Stasi - East German secret police - in Germany, and then failed to pay off the storage yard fees" (see article that follows)

Scurei paid the outstanding storage fees and had the slabs moved to his Phoenix backyard, which by de facto became a monument. He told Skip that one morning, as he was having a cup of coffee in his backyard garden, he noticed a big bus full of snooping onlookers right outside his house. It didn't take Scurei long to realize that they wanted to see the monument in his backyard.

Scurei did go back to East Berlin to find out the history and exact location of the three specific pieces. And because he had purchased the slabs to donate them to a school, when Skip suggested DLI as the potential recipient, Scurei immediately accepted the idea. Thus, for the last four years Skip has gone back and forth between Scurei and the Installation leadership, namely Colonels Kevin Rice, Michael Simone, and Jeffrey Cairns, to secure a place for the slabs at the Presidio of Monterey. Finally, in the last several months Skip worked with the DLI Memorialization Committee, who went thru all the necessary steps to put a closure to his proposal. At the end Col. Simone, the present DLI Commandant, funded the construction project for a Berlin Wall Memorial. Special credit should also be given to former DLI employees Cliff Porter and Arthur Douglas for the design and initial coordination of the Berlin Wall Memorialization Project.

According to the 2002 Herald's article, "the gift comes with three strings attached: Scurei wants the slabs used as a teaching tool about the Cold War and tolerance; the names of those who died trying to cross the wall are to be memorialized; and his gift must be acknowledged."

As we all know, countless DLI graduates of Russian, German, Czech, Polish, and many other European languages served in Berlin and West Germany during the five decades of the Cold War. The best known is Major Arthur Nicholson, a DLI Russian graduate who bled to dead after being shot by a Soviet sentry in East Berlin. Building 848, Nicholson Hall, was named in his honor.

Details for an appropriate dedication ceremony are presently being discussed at the Installation and naturally, Walter Scurei and his family will be guests of honor at the celebration. Although nothing else is firm, the Alumni Relations Office suggested having the event close to 9 November 2005, the next anniversary of the Wall's collapse. The final arrangements will be formally released when approved by appropriate Installation officials. Therefore, stay tuned.

❖

Donna Kelly (third from right), DLI graduate of Russian, Polish, and Serbian-Croatian, brought her family for a visit to the Berlin Wall Monument in early 2014

Col. Tucker Mansager shakes hands with Mr. Walter Scurei, as brother Paul and sister Victoria look on

Berlin Wall Dedication Ceremony
Presidio of Monterey - November 2005
DLIAA Newsletter VII - July 2005

In May 2005, five years after Billy (Skip) Johnson's serendipitous sighting of three concrete slabs in Walter Scurei's backyard in Phoenix, Arizona, the three Berlin wall pieces were relocated and made into a historic monument at the Presidio of Monterey, California. Six months later, on November 9th, a spectacular ceremony was held at the Presidio to dedicate the monument. The dedication plaque, unveiled by Col. Tucker Mansager and the Scurei family, contains a commemorative inscription that pays tribute to:

> *"Those who fell trying to reach freedom,*
> *Those who fell preserving freedom, and*
> *All who served defending freedom."*

As thousands of DLI graduates are represented in the last two lines, in many respects this was a dedication to them, particularly all those who were assigned to Berlin during the five decades of the Cold War. While the Cold War played out around the world, the

Berlin Wall was perhaps the most visible manifestation of that five-decade long conflict. During those years, DLI graduates - cryptologists, intelligence personnel, Foreign Area Officers and others - served at U.S. Field Station Berlin as members of the U.S. Military Liaison Mission Potsdam, East Germany, and in other military and diplomatic positions requiring language skills around the world.

The dedication plaque also contains one of the most powerful lines uttered in recent American history, taken from President Reagan's speech at the Brandenburg Gate on June 12, 1987: *"Mr. Gorbachev, tear down this wall!"* This 2,703 words speech, addressed to West Berliners, could also be heard on the east side of the Wall.

The ceremony was presided by Col. Tucker Mansager, current Installation Commander and DLI Commandant, who soon after his arrival this last August (2005), put the stamp of approval on the event, initiated during the tenures of Col. Jeffrey Cairns, Garrison Commander, and Col. Kevin Rice (ret), the preceding DLI Commandant.

Dozens of dignitaries were present at the observance. They included Mr. Edwin Meese, attorney general in President Ronald Reagan's administration, the mayors and city managers of the surrounding communities.

Special invitation was extended to Mr. and Mrs. Walter Scurei, his brother Paul and sister Victoria, as well as various members of his family who flew from Arizona to attend the historic event. Mr. Scurei had donated to DLI the three pieces, which he had bought from an Arizona warehouse after they had been stored there and *"abandoned by an Arizona based hotel tycoon, who purchased them for $100,000 in 1990 as an investment from Stasi – East German secret police – in Germany, and then failed to pay off the storage yard fees"* (quoted from a Monterey Herald article). When Skip Johnson, DLI's assistant IG, visited his sister in Phoenix, he met one of her neighbors, Scurei, and upon seeing the three slabs in the latter's backyard discovered their origin and found out that Scurei planned to donate them to an educational institution. It didn't take long for Johnson to convince Scurei that DLI was the perfect final location for the monument. In his speech to the Institute's audience, Mr. Scurei stated that *"For 28 years, the Berlin Wall, 93 jagged* miles of concrete and barbed wire, cut the city of Berlin apart. The Berlin Wall was unique: Instead of keeping adversaries out, it imprisoned Berlin's own citizens and the citizens of the Eastern Bloc. For 28 years, more than 5,000 people made their escape, and more than 3,200 were arrested in the attempt to escape."

The occasion would not have been complete without the presence of the man who inserted the famous *"tear down this wall"* line in Reagan's speech, Mr. Peter Robinson, a research fellow at the Hoover Institution who was at the time the president's speech writer. Robinson stated that the entire White House apparatus as well as the State department wanted the line expunged from the speech. However, the president prevailed; the line was left in, and became history. In describing the story of the famous quote he indicated that the speech had gone through staffing for several weeks before the President delivered it, and that the entire foreign policy apparatus of the United States government had fought it. At one point, he said that the deputy chief of staff, Ken Duberstein *"felt he had no choice but to take the matter back to the President for a final decision. He sat the President down in the garden of an Italian palazzo, picking knee-deep the central passage in the speech, excising all the arguments against it and then talked it over with him.* Robinson wasn't present at that meeting, but Ken Duberstein told him what happened. They talked about it for a while and then Ken said he saw a twinkle of a light come into the President's eyes. Ronald Reagan said, *"Now, I'm the President, aren't I?"*- *"Yes, Mr. President, we're clear about that."* - *"So, I get to decide if that line stays in."* - *"Sir, it is your decision."* - *"Well then, it stays in"*, said Reagan.

Robinson said that on the day the party flew to Berlin, the State Department faxed over yet another alternative draft, omitting that one sentence about tearing down the Wall. In the limousine on the way to the Wall, to deliver the speech, the President signified that he was sticking to the original language. Then he moved across the limousine and slapped Duberstein on the knee and said, *"The boys at State aren't going to like this very much, but it's the right thing to do."* Robinson added that "*largely because Ronald Reagan did the right thing, we have these three ugly but beautiful slabs of concrete here today , no longer in Berlin as a monument to an evil empire, but here in Monterey as a monument to American determination."*

The Deputy German Consul General in San Francisco, Dr. Christian Seebode, was a special invitee who also spoke at the ceremony. He placed the construction of the wall in historical perspective, adding that *"nobody would have believed in fact that this symbol of the Cold War could or would come down. One of the political lessons we, all of us, Germans and the Americans as well, have learned from this is that nothing between heaven and earth is impossible if you firmly believe in your objectives and strive to reach them at the right time, and with the right means."*

The 100 person audience also heard from the DLI Chancellor, Dr. Donald Fischer. From 1989 to 1992, Fischer served a tour as DLI Commandant. Prior to that assignment, Fischer had commanded a missile air defense battalion in Bad Kreuznach, (West) Germany, where he served 16 years of his Army career. Events accelerated in East Germany during Fischer's DLI tour so that by the time he retired in 1992 the world had been transformed in amazing ways. At the conclusion of his speech, Fischer directed his remarks to current DLI language students, stating that *"The new generation of students that has to deal with languages and cultures is far different and with much different goals than we had to deal with. To those students, I say that the torch is now passed to you. I envy your youth, I envy your challenge, and it is my hope that in a few years, there will be another monument here to your efforts, complete with the success and the provisions of opportunity that these slabs from the Berlin Wall represent today."*

In his remarks Col. Tucker Mansager stated that he had *"served in Berlin as an infantry lieutenant from 1986 to 1989, where our nickname was "the Defenders of Freedom."* He added that *"in Berlin, as an incentive to reenlist Army soldiers in the mid-1980s, the reenlisting soldier was allowed to choose the place where he would take the oath to defend the Constitution of the United States. Perhaps the most moving reenlistments I have ever done were on the platform overlooking the Wall by the Brandenburg Gate, -- the very site where President Reagan stood to deliver his speech. We planted the biggest American flag we could carry to reinforce all those around the U.S. commitment to a free Berlin by extension of freedom everywhere. Another moving reenlistment location was the Freedom Bridge, over which Cold War prisoners, such as Francis Gary Powers, were exchanged and where the remains of DLI graduate*

Maj. Arthur Nicholson, killed by a Soviet soldier in East Germany, was returned to U.S. custody. We marched to the middle of this bridge and planted the U.S. colors on the line of the middle of the bridge that separated freedom from tyranny. This was an attempt in a small way to show that we were indeed 'The Defenders of Freedom.'"

As the fall of the Berlin Wall represents a particular defining moment in two countries histories, the November ceremony started with the American and German national anthems. A senior NCO of German descent, 1st Sergeant Frank Everson, performed the master of ceremonies duties, and Installation chaplain Gianstefano Martin gave the invocation in English and German. After the speeches by colonel Mansager, Mr. Robinson, the Deputy German Consul General, and Dr. Fischer, the formal ceremony was followed by a photo session and interviews by the local press.

Subsequently, the DLI Alumni Association held an informal reception at Nakamura Hall Auditorium, where the German department choir sang several German songs and a group of Serbian/Croatian students entertained the audience with East European dances. Before and after the entertainment, the cheerful audience could watch a slide show portraying the transport of the slabs from Scurei's backyard to their present location at the Presidio of Monterey. While tasting light hors d'ouvres and listening to John Philip Sousa marches, the ceremony concluded as the guests exchanged stories, said goodbye to each other, and one by one went their separate ways.

One could tell by the comments of the gathered guests that this was one of the most memorable and impressive ceremonies in their memory. It is quite evident that the Institute is eternally grateful to Walter, Paul, and Victoria Scurei for this magnificent contribution to the Institute, representing an everlasting monument to the achievements of the countless alumni who served in Europe during the Cold War.

❖

Plaque donated by the DLI Alumni Association is displayed at the May 2006 Memorial Day parade.

MEMORIAL DAY AND WAR ACCOUNTS

Memorial Day parade honors 13 DLIFLC graduates killed in action

DLIAA Newsletter XI – July 2006

Following a long American tradition, the Defense Language Institute Foreign Language Center, DLIFLC, celebrated Memorial Day, this year on Thursday, 25 May. This federal holiday began first to honor Union soldiers who died during the American Civil War. After World War I, it expanded to include those who died in any war or military action.

Ever since the first DLIFLC graduation of 45 Japanese students in May 1942, from the then called Military Intelligence Service Military School, MISLS, the Institute has seen thousands of its graduates participate in all the military conflicts from World War II to the present.

Nine MISLS men were killed in action during World War II, and another 15 died in non-battle related incidents during that war. Although we do not know how many graduates were killed in action in Korea, we know that several hundred MISLS and Army

Language School, ALS, graduates served in that conflict. In Vietnam the Institute lost 295 of its graduates. Their names have been memorialized on several plaques now displayed in the DLIFLC headquarters building. Unfortunately, no accurate count was kept of DLIFLC graduates who lost their lives during the Cold War or in the several struggles from Grenada, Panama, Somalia, Bosnia, to the First Gulf War. However, in the last several decades, eleven graduates from all the conflicts since WWII have been honored with the names of Presidio buildings.

DLFLC Memorial Day parade on 25 May was an appropriate opportunity to honor all wars dead, and was specially arranged to render tribute to 13 DLIFLC alumni who were killed in action since September 11th, 2001. The commemorating bronze plaque reads: TO DLIFLC GRADUATES KILLED AS A RESULT OF HOSTILE ACTION IN THE WAR ON TERROR". The plaque was unveiled by Col. Tucker Mansager, DLIFLC Installation Commander, Command Sgt. Major (CSM) Nicholas Rozumny, Col. Joseph Ameel (U.S. Army, retired), guest speaker, and Mr. Benjamin De La Selva, DLI Alumni Association, DLIAA, President.

The military ceremony was a magnificent and solemn occasion that included a stimulating speech, a 3-volley salute, a roll call, and the presence of two close relatives of the fallen alumni.

Col. Tucker Mansager set the commemoration backdrop with inspiring words and recognized the presence of several special guests, who included Lisa Vance, the wife of West Virginia National Guard Staff Sergeant Gene A. Vance Jr., and Gena Nason, sister of Chief Warrant Officer 2, Christopher G. Nason.

Col. Ameel, the occasion guest speaker who served two tours in Vietnam, gave prudent advice to the young servicemen in the parade field and in the stands. Among several suggestions he told DLIFLC students to always expect the unexpected in combat, to keep up their language skills and to learn the customs and cultures of other countries.

The roll call was conducted from the stage podium by CSM Rozumny, who first called out the rank and name of three servicemen present at the parade. After each was recognized by name, each serviceman responded: "Here, Sergeant Major". Then, the name of the 13 fallen graduates was called one by one, three times: first by rank and last name, then by rank, first name, and last name, and finally by rank and full name. As the Sergeant Major read on, many of the attendees glanced at the names on the Memorial Day program. Obviously moved, the audience grew and remained quiet until the end of the ceremony. Hearing out loud the names of the fallen had a powerful yet sobering effect on them.

The roll call was followed by a 3-volley salute, a ceremony normally performed at military funerals. On this occasion, three soldiers, each with an M-16 rifle, fired their weapons in unison three times at short intervals, for a total of 9 shots. To conclude the ceremony, the military bugle call "Taps" was sounded. Taps in the U.S. military is generally sounded at funerals and memorial services.

DLIFLC plans to add the names of future linguist heroes at each year's Memorial Day remembrance. Upon knowledge of any such demise, readers are ask to submit names of fallen heroes to the DLIFLC PAO office with as much information as possible, for possible inclusion in the memorial.

Mounted on a carefully polished wooden board and displaying 13 brass name plates, the commemorating bronze plaque was donated by the DLI Alumni Association (www.dli-alumni.org), who raised the funds from membership donations and DLI memorabilia sales. The plaque is on display on the second floor of Rasmussen Hall, the DLIFLC headquarters.

In Memoriam
DLIFLC GRADUATES KILLED AS A RESULT OF HOSTILE ACTION IN THE WAR ON TERROR

• **David A. Defeo**, 37, a Polish linguist, class of 1983, an employee of Sandler O'Neil, was the first casualty. He died in the attack on the New York World Trade Center on Sept. 11, 2001.
• **Staff Sgt. Gene Arden Vance Jr.**, 38, a Persian-Farsi linguist, class of 1998, serving with 2nd Battalion, 19th Special Forces Group of the West Virginia Army National Guard, was killed by enemy small arms fire in Afghanistan on May 19, 2002.
• **Army CW3 Mark Steven Osteen**, 43, a Spanish linguist, class of 1986, serving with D Company, 1st Battalion, 160th Special

Operations Air Reconnaissance unit, was killed in an air crash in Afghanistan Jan. 30, 2003.

Navy Petty Officer 1st Class David Martin Tapper, 32, a Persian-Farsi linguist, class of 1997, was serving with the Commander, Naval Special Warfare Group, when he was killed by enemy small arms fire in Afghanistan Aug. 20, 2003.
• **Army Specialist Alyssa Renee Peterson**, 27, an Arabic linguist, class of 2003, serving with Company C of the 101st Airborne Division's 311th Military Intelligence Battalion, died of a gunshot wound in Telafar, Iraq, Sept. 16, 2003.

Army CW2 Christopher Gregg Nason, 29, an Arabic linguist, class of 1996, was killed in a vehicle accident Nov. 23, 2003, while serving with the 306th Military Intelligence Battalion in Iraq.
• **Marine Corps Gunnery Sgt. Ronald Eric Baum**, 38, a Spanish linguist, class of 1994, was killed by an improvised explosive device in Iraq on May 3, 2004, while serving with the 2nd Intelligence Battalion, 2nd Marine Division, 2nd Marine Expeditionary Force.
• **Navy Petty Officer 1st Class Brian Joseph Ouellette**, 37, a Spanish linguist, class of 1996, was killed by an improvised explosive device May 29, 2004, while serving with Navy Special Warfare Group 2 in Kandahar, Afghanistan.

• **Jamie M. Michalsky**, 24, a Russian linguist, class of 2000. was killed by a suicide bomber while working as a civilian with Worldwide Language Resources in Kabul, Afghanistan, Oct. 23, 2004.
• **Army Sgt. Joseph Michael Nolan**, 27, an Arabic linguist, class of 2002, was killed Nov. 18, 2004, by an improvised explosive device in Baghdad while serving with C Company of the 101st Airborne Division's 311th Military Intelligence Battalion.

• **Army Sgt. Cari Anne Gasiewicz**, 28, an Arabic linguist, class of 2003, was killed by an improvised explosive device Dec. 4, 2004, while serving with B Company, 202nd Military Intelligence Battalion, 513th Military Intelligence Brigade, in Ba'qubah, Iraq.
• **Navy Senior Chief Petty Officer Daniel Richard Healy**, 36, a

Russian linguist, class of 1997, was killed in a plane crash in Afghanistan June 28, 2005.

• **Army Reserve Sgt. Myla Lumayag Maravillosa**, 24, a Tagalog linguist, class of 2003, was killed by an improvised explosive device Dec. 24, 2005 while serving with the 203rd Military Intelligence Battalion in Iraq.

Note: From 2006 to 2014, nineteen more service members were added to the plaque:

Name	Date	Country
1LT Scott M. Love	7 Jun 06	Iraq
CPL Bernard P. Corpuz	11 Jun 06	Afghanistan
SSGT Kyu H. Chay	28 Oct 06	Afghanistan
LTC Eric J. Kruger	2 Nov 06	Iraq
CPT Travis L.S. Patriquin	6 Dec 06	Iraq
SFC Sean K. Mitchell	7 Jul 07	Mali
CPT Michael A. Norman	31 Jan 08	Iraq
CPO Nathah H. Hardy	4 Feb 08	Iraq
1LT Jason D. Mann	17 Jul 08	Afghanistan
MSG Anthony Davis	25 Nov 08	Iraq
SGT Andrew J. Creighton	4 Jul 10	Afghanistan
CPT Lucas T. Pyeatt	5 Feb 11	Afghanistan
LT COL Frank Bryant Jr.	27 Apr 11	Afghanistan
SFC Terry L. Pasker	9 Jul 11	Afghanistan
SSG Michael W. Hobby	17 Sep 11	Afghanistan
SRA Julian Sholten	18 Feb 12	Africa
LT COL John D. Loftis	25 Feb 12	Afghanistan
SSGT Richard A. Dickson	27 Apr 13	Afghanistan
SPC Christopher A. Landis	10 Feb 14	Afghanistan

Michael Landolfi   David Villareal

A Tale of two Linguists
An effort to rectify a Gulf War account
DLIAA Newsletter XII – October 2006

MICHAEL LANDOLFI. The years 1990 and 1991 were not the best or the worst of times for Michael Landolfi, a native of Santa Rosa, California. In April 1990 he successfully graduated from the prestigious Defense Language Institute Foreign Language Center, after undergoing 47 grueling weeks of studying Modern Standard Arabic and another 16 weeks of learning the Egyptian dialect.

After a few weeks with the 101st Airborne in Fort Campbell, Kentucky, Landolfi was deployed to Iraq in February 1991, to the first Gulf War as an Arabic translator, to the front lines. As the only linguist "officially" attached to the 1st Battalion, 187th Infantry Regiment, he was performing standard tactical duties of a combat unit linguist, i.e., prisoner interrogation, document exploitation, liaison work with other units, etcetera.

In one of those "fine" exhausting afternoons, an Associated Press reporter came into the Regiment's area looking for the Arabic linguist who was responsible for the recent surrender of 450 Iraqi soldiers. Mistakenly, the reporter was escorted to Landolfi's tent to meet the unit's "linguist." The reporter, naturally, proceeded to interview Landolfi at some length and just assumed that he was talking to the one and only linguist on location.

As it happened, the reporter had already heard the details of the deed, and assuming Landolfi was the one who "scored" the massive prisoner surrender, did not verify if Landolfi was the central figure of the story, but assumed this was the case, and merely glossed over the information offered to him during the interview.

Landolfi did not find out for some time that both the *Associated Press* and the *Army Times* had published articles with the mistaken information. The headline in the *Associated Press* article, dated Feb 28th, 1991 read: "MEGAPHONE WAS PRIME WEAPON FOR ARMY'S ARABIC SPEAKER - Specialist Michael Landolfi's main weapon wasn't an M-16. It was a megaphone."

The article went on to say that Landolfi had helped his unit to induce more than 450 Iraqi soldiers to surrender by using a megaphone from an Apache helicopter gunship. Supposedly, Michael told the soldiers (in Arabic) they would be killed if they didn't give up.

The Army Times had published the account as part of special Desert Storm issue entitled "HOW WE KICKED HIS BUTT," dated 11 March 1991, page 36, "51st Year, No. 32." The AT article was somewhat shorter and contained the sub headline "Surrender Specialist," but basically contained the same information.

Unsure on how to go about it, Landolfi for years had been intending to rectify the reported story. In an email to the DLI Alumni Association (DLIAA) in September 2003 he stated: *"It's ironic: I am currently a graduate student in history at Catholic University and have become acutely aware of the need for an accurate historical record, yet I myself am at the center of sloppy reporting and an incorrect account! Has this tale become part of "official" DLI folklore? If so, I should probably contact the POM (Presidio of Monterey) historian and give him the real story..."*

But Landolfi became busy with other issues in life and somehow the story "fell" on the back burner, and he himself disappeared from DLIAA's radar screen when he changed his email address. With a stroke of luck, recent DLIAA attempts to reach Landolfi succeeded and the "megaphone surrender" story has been retold, perhaps the right way this time.

But our story is not over yet. In a bizarre twist, the true hero of this incredible feat has come to the forefront, "hiding" in the mist of DLIFLC itself!

DAVID VILLAREAL. David Villarreal, a native of Bovina, Texas, was the unheard-of champion whose name had been shrouded in anonymity. Though Landolfi had identified him as one of the other linguists assigned to the 101st to the Associated Press reporter, Villarreal remained anonymous, that is, until this very moment.

Villarreal first arrived at DLIFLC in July 1988 and 63 weeks later, in November 1989, graduated from the Modern Standard and Egyptian dialect basic course. Similarly to Landolfi, Villarreal reported to 311th MI BN, 101st Airborne Division in Fort Campbell, Kentucky and was preparing for deployment when Saddam Hussein invaded Kuwait on August 2, 1990, triggering a United States' response known as Operation Desert Shield.

In what became known as the First Gulf War, Villarreal was assigned to Bravo Company, 1st Battalion, 187th Infantry Regiment, 101st Airborne Division and was immediately deployed to Kuwait along with another dozen Arabic linguists.

With the beginning of the ground war in late January 1991, many of the initial assaults were carried out by paratroopers in UH-60 Blackhawk helicopters, with Apache Gunship helicopters flying around as air support.

As the story goes, in one of these air assaults, Villarreal and several other linguists rushed into the area as support combat troops and found many Iraqi soldiers walking around somewhat confused. Villarreal's Company Commander handed him a megaphone and told him to talk to the soldiers in Arabic. The message they received was clear: "If you do not give up immediately, you will be annihilated." The result was the surrender of 450 Iraqi soldiers. For his performance with the 187th Villarreal received an Army Commendation Medal (ARCOM).

"When it happened, we laughed about it," said Villarreal. "I remember that Landolfi called his family and told them what had really happened...and I didn't care...I thought it was exciting to have done it and it was a good story, no matter who got the credit."

Villarreal went back to Fort Campbell in April 1991, but within several years, found himself yet again on another assignment in Iraq with the 3rd Armored Cavalry Regiment (ACR) in 2003.

And so, in the end, the real hero was recognized for being the protagonist of the feat. In all honesty, Landolfi thinks Villarreal should have received a higher award than an ARCOM for the extraordinary deed alone.

Where are they now? Landolfi is a civilian and currently works for the United States Government on the East Coast. Villarreal is a Sergeant First Class serving as Chief Military Language Instructor with Middle East III School, Defense Language Institute, Monterey, California.

"The 1st Gulf War was very different than the second," said Villarreal, speaking in his Presidio office with schedules, numbers and names scribbled all over the white boards behind him. "Soldiers now have more interaction with Iraqi people as the mission is a more humanitarian one in nature."

He said that students are expected to graduate from DLIFLC with a higher proficiency rate than ever, as their skills are more crucial to the success of troops deployed. "Students have to learn more than we did back in my day."

DLIFLC responds to Operation Desert Shield linguistic needs

DLI *GLOBE* - September 1990

Soon after the onset of Operation Desert Shield, the calls to the Defense Language Institute for support began pouring into the Middle East School and the Nonresident Training Division. Shortly thereafter, Col. Donald C. Fischer, DLI commandant, set up and operation center headed by Col. William K. Olds, DLI School Secretary, to serve as a planning body and a clearing house for all the requests from the field. The first needed support was translation requests, followed by requests for course materials and tapes for units wanting to brush up on the Iraqi dialect.

On August 18, a battalion commander at Fort Campbell, Kentucky, called Fischer to request training assistance with the Iraqi dialect for 70 linguists of his battalion. By 4 p.m. the next day, Sunday, DLI had reached several Iraqi instructors from within and without the Institute to form a mobile training team, MTT.

One instructor flew to Fort Campbell early the following morning and undertook the Herculean task of giving Iraqi dialect familiarization to the battalion linguists who support the "Screaming Eagles" of World War II and Vietnam fame. "I taught groups of ten soldiers every two hours from 7 to 11 a.m. and from noon to 6 p.m. every day, including Saturday. Then, in the evening, I had to prepare for the following day", said the instructor, obviously tired.

After the instructor finished each two hour session, the linguists received instruction via Video Tele-training, VTT, from Fort Ord.

There, the DLI team of three other DLI instructors, plus two retirees on contract, prepared and delivered tailored Iraqi interrogation scenarios to the soldiers. The assistant division commander and the battalion commander were thoroughly impressed and profusely praised the two week MTT-VTT combination effort.

Even before the operation, without knowing, DLI began supporting the future *Desert Shield* in July when the 337th MI Battalion, Melbourne, Fla., requested refresher training for 11 Arabic linguists. Venus Attia, Arabic instructor and DLI educational Technology and staff, went to Florida to give them face to face and computer-based instruction. Some of those reservists have already been activated and are ready to deploy to Saudi Arabia.

A week after the DLI *Desert Shield* operations center was established, Fischer and selected DLI employees provided Under Secretary of the Army, John Shannon, a timely briefing on the assistance DLI was rendering in support of *Operation Desert Shield*. Additionally, Fischer presented Shannon three DLI-conceived contingency options: 1) Provide Iraqi dialect training to existing MOS-qualified Arabic linguists. 2) Divert current DLI students undergoing other dialects into the Iraqi dialect. 3) Increase the Iraqi dialect training program.

DLI recently sent a message to the Training and Doctrine Command costing out each of the options. Assistance will continue in terms of MTT's and VTT's and has already expanded with telephone testing of reservists who claim speaking proficiency in Arabic. Tough these undertakings have already put some strain on the Middle East School, the Arabic faculty has responded quickly and enthusiastically to all the taskings.

DLI-West Coast Branch Graduates Killed as a Result of Hostile Action in Vietnam

Taken from the graduation program of the last Vietnamese class held at DLIFLC, 21 October 2004.

CAPT Leon J. Kramer, 31 Jan 63
1LT Parker D. Cramer, 6 May 63
CPT Curtis J. Steckbauer, 1 Jul 63
1LT Donald C. Johansen, 20 Oct 63
SFC Chester D. Townsend, 1 Dec 63
SFC David Thompson, 27 Jan 64
CPT Jerry L. Taylor, 17 Feb 64
CAPT Thomas J. Bergin, 14 Mar 64
CAPT James P. Spruill, 21 Apr 64
1LT Ronald D.J. Hines, 26 Apr 64
MAJ Arnold D. Kniffin, 1 Jun 64
1LT Ralph G. Redmond, 4 Jun 64
SFC Thomas Maultsby Jr., 10 Jul 64
CAPT Billy T. Hatfield, 13 Jul 64
CAPT Richard M. Stroka, 13 Jul 64
CAPT James J. McClain, 28 Jul 64
CAPT Dale D. Thomas, 30 Jul 64
SSG Wilfrid N. Bourgeois, 17 Aug 64
CAPT James M. Coyle, 20 Aug 64
CPT William D.H. Ragin, 20 Aug 64
CAPT Byron C. Stone, 20 Aug 64
CAPT Robert J. Reilly, 11 Oct 64
CAPT Herman Towery, 22 Oct 64
LT COL Thomas Whitlock, 1 Nov 64
CAPT Heriberto A. Garcia, 8 Nov 64
SFC Donald E. Smith, 13 Nov 64
MAJ Roy E. Congleton, 21 Dec 64
SSGT Gerard A. Binger, 22 Jan 65
CAPT Elvis G. Barker, 1 Mar 65
CPT Alvin K. Broyles Jr., 28 Apr 65
CAPT John C. Sigg, 28 May 65
MSG Hugh M. Robbins, 1 Jun 65
SWF2 William C. Hoover, 10 Jun 65
SFC Fred M. Owens, 10 Jun 65
CAPT Eugene D. Franklin, 24 Jun 65
SFC Alfred H. Combs Jr., 25 Jun 65
SFC Henry Alfred Musa Jr., 5 Jul 65
SSG Herbert Smith Jr., 8 Jul 65
CAPT Robert J. Voss, 8 Jul 65
SP5 Stanley P. Kierzek, 20 Jul 65
CAPT James C. Caston, 10 Aug 65
CAPT Robert H. Fuellhart, 12 Aug 65
SFC Thomas H. Betts, 4 Sep 65
MAJ Herbert J. Dexter, 18 Sep 65
SSGT David A. Morgan, 23 Sep 65
SSGT Daniel C. Chappell, 28 Oct 65
1LT William J. Lyons, 4 Nov 65
COL George McCutchen, 20 Nov 65
MAJ Raymond Celeste, 22 Nov 65
CAPT William R. McPherson, 3 Dec 65
1SG James P. Tyner, 8 Jan 66
SSG Donald L. Dotson, 29 Jan 66
MAJ Daniel M. Martz Jr., 12 Feb 66
CAPT Lyell F. King, 18 Feb 66
CPT William A. Stacy Jr., 21 Mar 66
MAJ James B. Conway, 12 Apr 66

PVT Grant C. Taylor, 5 Jun 67
LCPL Victor L. Burns, 27 Jun 67
CPT Graham N. Lowdon Jr., 28 Jun 67
PFC Kevin G. O'Connell, 29 Jun 67
LCPL Glenn E. Sanders, 29 Jun 67
PFC Terri L. Hines, 2 Jul 67
MAJ John M. Kessinger, 2 Jul 67
LCPL Terry L. Quigley, 2 Jul 67
1LT Anthony J. Borrego, 5 Jul 67
LCPL John W. Granahan, 5 Jul 67
LCPL Richard R. Davis, 7 Jul 67
LCPL Richard H. Lopez, 7 Jul 67
LCPL Michael Boardman, 19 Jul 67
LCPL Richard J. Behrns, 23 Jul 67
PFC Roderick L. Weiss, 24 Jul 67
CPT Arthur H. Green, 3 Aug 67
LCPL Robert I. Klootwyk, 8 Aug 67
CPL Vernon Thorsteinson, 12 Aug 67
LCPL David M. Calabria, 17 Aug 67
PFC Jack E. Telling, 4 Sep 67
LCPL James M. Daniels, 7 Sep 67
LCPL Robert R. Rogers, 7 Sep 67
CPL Robert M. Warren, 7 Sep 67
CPT Thomas D. Culp, 11 Sep 67
PFC John O. Kerney, 13 Sep 67
LCPL Duane J. Foss, 14 Oct 67
MAJ John O. Cooper III, 26 Oct 67
CPL Nicholas B. Enriquez, 1 Nov 67
CPT Michael A. Crabtree, 18 Nov 67
CPT David J. Decker, 19 Nov 67
CPT Harold J. Kaufman, 20 Nov 67
SP5 Michael P. Brown, 26 Nov 67
MAJ Antonio Mauroudis, 28 Nov 67
LCPL Thomas McElynn, 30 Nov 67
MAJ Charles D. Wilkie, 8 Dec 67
MSG Edward K. Robison, 3 Jan 68
LT Richard O. Williams, 5 Jan 68
MAJ Lawrence M. Malone, 7 Jan 68
PFC William A. Markarian, 7 Jan 68
LCPL Thomas N. Brewer, 7 Jan 68
CPL David N. Nicholson, 8 Jan 68
CPL Philip F. Burrell, 11 Jan 68
1LT Alfred B. Russ, 13 Jan 68
CPL Roger L. Wilson, 20 Jan 68
PFC Michael D. Cruitt, 21 Jan 68
CPT Daniel W. Kent, 24 Jan 68
MAJ Francis G. Gercz Jr., 25 Jan 68
SSG Gary L. Crone, 29 Jan 68
CPL Callen B. Courtemanche, 31 Jan 68
MSGT Marvin J. Plata, 31 Jan 68
CPL Robert E. Hall, 3 Feb 68
GYSGT George P. Kendall Jr., 4 Feb 68
LTC Vorin E. Whan, 7 Feb 68
CPT Howard L. Jaouen, 8 Feb 68
CPT Sidney L. Leonard, 10 Feb 68
CPT Felix Sosa-Camejo, 13 Feb 68

PFC Peter W. Sobacki, 10 Sep 68
PFC Harold J. Mathews Jr., 11 Sep 68
MAJ Alvin G. Mutter, 14 Sep 68
PFC Edward Cunningram, 16 Sep 68
MAJ Norman Cunningham, 24 Sep 68
MSG Antonio B. Jaime, 5 Oct 68
LCPL Al D. Corbo, 13 Oct 68
MAJ Thomas J. Baker, 4 Nov 68
LCPL Lawrence J. Putz Jr., 25 Nov 68
SP6 Allen I. Limbreck, 22 Dec 68
LTC Thomas F. O'Dea, 25 Dec 68
LCPL Jon M. Rumble, 26 Dec 68
SFC James C. Nicholson, 2 Jan 69
MAJ William Elsten, 5 Jan 69
PFC Deane F. Smith, 8 Jan 69
LCPL William C. Ingram, 22 Jan 69
SSG Bruce E. Deerinwater, 25 Jan 69
PFC Robert W. Whitney, 16 Feb 69
LCPL Dennis J. Kane, 17 Feb 69
CPL John P. Cook, 18 Feb 69
CPT Lee R. Herron, 22 Feb 69
CPL Bruce E. Robinson, 22 Feb 69
LTC William W. Dickey, 23 Feb 69
CPL Roger M. Kittleson, 25 Feb 69
CPT Ronald M. Goulet, 26 Feb 69
LCPL Martin R. Powers, 27 Feb 69
LCPL Philip H. Marks, 16 Mar 69
LTC Albert C. Butler, 22 Mar 69
LCPL Michael R. Ball, 26 Mar 69
SFC Arthur M. Bradberry, 30 Mar 69
MSGT John E. Lewis, 16 Apr 69
SFC William F. Rocco, 23 Apr 69
SFC Robert L. King, 25 Apr 69
LCPL David L. Girardo, 3 May 69
SFC Kenneth L. Dulley, 6 May 69
PFC Robert J. Alert Jr., 9 May 69
PFC Richard D. Cheney, 9 May 69
CPT Gerald Wrazen, 14 May 69
MSGT Bruce I. Luttrell, 20 May 69
CPL Albert J. Cartledge, 27 May 69
SSG John M. Blackford, 7 Jun 69
PFC Larry C. Bradborn, 7 Jun 69
LCPL Robert V. Reker, 13 Jun 69
SSG Gerald K. Neer, 17 Jun 69
CPT James R. Daniel, 19 Jun 69
CPT Anton W. Boroski, 26 Jun 69
LCPL Patrick R. Scott, 6 Jul 69
LTC Arnold C. Hayward, 11 Jul 69
SP4 George J. Pascale, 14 Jul 69
LCPL John S. Kraabel, 18 Jul 69
CPL Michael C. Wunsch, 28 Jul 69
PFC Bruce W. Carter, 7 Aug 69
PFC Charles Velasquez, 13 Aug 69
MSG Chalmers Humphreys, 17 Aug 69
LCPL Charles B. Walker Jr., 3 Sep 69

CPT Burton K. McCord, 14 Apr 66
CPT Joseph J. Polonko Jr., 29 Apr 66
SFC John J. Dewers, 5 May 66
SFC Thomas H. Welsh, 16 May 66
CPT John E. Dieckmann, 18 May 66
LTC Ernest E. Lane Jr., 18 May 66
MAJ Gunther W. Norberg, 7 Jun 66
CPT Michael J. Soth, 21 Jun 66
CPT Humbert R. Versace, 1 Jul 66
MAJ Edwin J. MacNamera, 3 Jul 66
CPT Sherrill V. Brown, 10 Jul 66
MSG Henry H. Delano, 22 Jul 66
MSG Clarence L. Sexton, 30 Jul 66
CPT Gary L. Vinas, 13 Aug 66
CPT Don T. Elledge, 18 Aug 66
MAJ Joseph B. Mack Jr., 17 Sep 66
PFC John W. Jarrell, 13 Oct 66
SGT John B. Geisen Jr., 26 Oct 66
CPL David A. Baruth, 27 Oct 66
LTC William C. Barott, 4 Nov 66
CPT Gerald F. Currier, 4 Nov 66
CPT Bernard S. Plaza, 23 Nov 66
1LT Daniel M. Kellett, 8 Dec 66
MAJ John H. Joyce, 21 Dec 66
CPT Roy M. McWilliams, 20 Jan 67
CPT Hardy W. Peeples, 21 Jan 67
CPT Charles M. Titus, 28 Jan 67
SSG Theodore H. Davis, 26 Feb 67
CPT Nelson S. Lehman Jr., 7 Mar 67
CPT Thomas F. Sauble, 13 Mar 67
MSG Charles E. Hosking Jr., 21 Mar 67
LCPL Leigh W. Hunt, 24 Mar 67
CPT Thomas P. Mitchell, 26 Mar 67
CPT Daniel F. Monahan, 14 Apr 67
PFC Bruce C. Parmalee, 21 Apr 67
LTC Charles J. Tighe, 23 Apr 67
CPT William A. Crenshaw, 4 May 67
CPT Joseph C. Hailey, 14 May 67
CPT Gerald A. Brown, 16 May 67
LTC Edward R. Frank Sr., 18 May 67
SSG Pedro A. Cruz, 22 May 67
CPT Joseph A. Tomko, 1 Jun 67
2LT Straughan Kelsey Jr., 3 Jun 67

LCPL Joe M. Copeland, 20 Feb 68
LTC James R. Etheridge, 23 Feb 68
CPT Daniel R. Schueren, 25 Feb 68
SSG Joe S. Rodriguez, 29 Feb 68
SSG Stephen J. Bobkovich, 1 Mar 68
LTC William C. DeLapp III, 8 Mar 68
CPL Keith M. Flumere, 11 Mar 68
LCPL Roger T. Nelson, 15 Mar 68
LTC Howard P. Petty, 15 Mar 68
SSG Billie O. Kean, 16 Mar 68
PFC Charles E. McMullin, 17 Mar 68
LCPL Billy Roy Bowen, 18 Mar 68
LCPL David L. Brown, 18 Mar 68
1SG Alan R. Haugen, 6 Apr 68
CPT William J. Whitehead, 7 Apr 68
PVT Robert J. Marcantoni, 10 Apr 68
CPL P.G. McGarvey, 12 Apr 68
CPL R.C. McMackins Jr., 14 Apr 68
LCPL Jerry F. Garcia, 17 Apr 68
CPL S.G. Schauermann, 30 Apr 68
LCPL W.B. Foard, 2 May 68
CPL Allen R. Bradford, 7 May 68
PFC Larry Stern, 25 May 68
CPT H.L. Haley, 26 May 68
CPL Craig B. Holt, 26 May 68
LCPL Gary C. Shafer, 27 May 68
LCPL Jeffery E. Feser, 5 Jun 68
PFC James R. Michael, 13 Jun 68
PFC R.D. Conklin, 15 Jun 68
LCPL Bernard F. Dutton Jr., 4 Jul 68
CPT John B. Reed, 4 Jul 68
CPL Richard S. Brown, 5 Jul 68
CPL John W. Hansard III, 15 Jul 68
CPT David G. Mitchell, 23 Jul 68
SSG Thomas G. Hudson, 5 Aug 68
PFC Donald M. Redmond, 10 Aug 68
CPL James O. Spaw, 18 Aug 68
LCPL Jerry A. Weimer, 23 Aug 68
1LT John E. Miller, 24 Aug 68
LTC Michael J. Ingrassia, 28 Aug 68
LCPL William L. Pitt, 28 Aug 68
CPL Ricky J. Almanza, 3 Sep 68
MSG Thomas W. Barnard, 8 Sep 68

LCPL John Chesebrough, 17 Sep 69
MAJ David R. Mackey, 17 Sep 69
PFC Allen T. Aslett, 27 Sep 69
SSGT Michael A. Piacentino, 28 Sep 69
CPL George A. Gillespie, 2 Nov 69
CPT Robert C. Beckman, 11 Nov 69
1LT Charles V. Penn, 29 Nov 69
LCPL Douglas Young, 20 Dec 69
EML James C. Mitchell Jr., 8 Jan 70
MAJ Tedd M. Lewis, 9 Jan 70
CPL Michael R. James, 11 Jan 70
CPT Richard J. Sexton III, 15 Feb 70
LCPL Jack A. Zoodsma, 17 Feb 70
LTC George A. Finter, 28 Feb 70
SGT Ehrhard K. Pohl, 22 Mar 70
CPL James C. Carlin, 1 Apr 70
MAJ James A. Russ, 27 Apr 70
CPT Ron V. Gray, 27 Apr 70
CPT James M. Treesh, 3 May 70
SP6 Thomas T. Smith, 3 May 70
MAJ George E. Hussey, 4 May 70
SGT David W. Smith, 17 May 70
MAJ Shane N. Soldato, 23 May 70
CPT Robert L. McCurdy, 26 May 70
1LT Dale Reising, 29 May 70
SGT Joseph J. Smith, 1 Jun 70
SP4 Robert W. McDonald, 16 Jun 70
MG George W. Casey, 7 Jul 70
MAJ Kenneth P. Tanner, 23 Jul 70
CPT David R. Weigner, 27 Jul 70
MAJ Barry F. Graham, 3 Aug 70
SGT Paul Miller, 20 Aug 70
CPL Gary W. Jones, 23 Aug 70
SGT Arthur Fisher, 20 Nov 70
SSG Steven F. Johnson, 14 Dec 70
ENC Frank W. Bomar, 20 Dec 70
SGT David C. Johnson, 5 Feb 71
SFC Olan D. Coleman, 11 Feb 71
SP5 Gary P. Westcott, 30 Mar 72
CPT Charles L. Flott, 5 Jun 72
LTC Willey B. McBride, 19 Jun 72
CPL Michael C. Smartt, 31 Dec 72

LANGUAGE PROGRAMS

"Captain Blanco was Here" -
A brief account of DLI's Spanish program since the 1960s
DLIAA Newsletter III - July 2004

Were you here in the 1960s or early 70s as a Spanish student? Then you remember Captain Blanco, a character who appeared in the first dialogues of the Old Spanish course; that is, the course taught until 1975. In those days, a lesson (as in almost all DLI languages) was built around a lengthy dialogue and a reading selection, with attendant vocabulary and pattern drills. The course was organized around daily situations from which a grammatical sequence was derived. Yes, you witnessed the last vestiges of the audio-lingual method. Dialogue memorization, mechanical drills, and contrived (non-authentic) materials kept you busy during the day and part of the night. When you started the course you were issued a black 40-pound reel-to-reel tape recorder and a dozen or two tape reels containing, again, contrived materials. Authentic materials consisted of newspapers that the Spanish department obtained several months after their publication. Thus, authentic news was old news. As there was a dearth of materials, teachers had to create their own and presented them using one of the latest technologies, the overhead projector. You had to spend about one hour a day in the listening lab, repeating the same dialogue lines and mechanical drills piped in from reel-to-reel tapes through the teacher's console. In the early 70s, at the urging of the user agencies, the Spanish program was augmented by the Basic Course Enrichment Program (BCEP), which contained what is now known as "performance objectives" (transcription, summarizing, number dictation, translation, etc.) BCEP exercises were mainly used with students going to Goodfellow AFB to become cryptologists.

If you came in the mid-1970s, you experienced a new Spanish course, developed in the now defunct "DLI Systems Development Agency", created by Commandant Horne in the early 1970's to develop learning systems. There you met Doctor Buendia, Captain Perez, Major Vega and Major Anderson. This course broke away from the audio-lingual method in several ways. First it discontinued the memorization of long dialogues. Instead, each lesson was broken up into three or four parts called frames, or conversational exchanges. From each frame grammar and vocabulary were extracted. Although not a strict situational/ grammatical syllabus like the previous course, this new course still observed a certain grammatical sequence but was more oriented on themes. The course writers claimed that in this modular approach they would be able to remove one module and replace it with another without impacting on the rest of the course. The course writers still used typewriters in its development. The advent of the cassette tapes allowed students for the first time to carry their recorders from the barracks to the school and do some of the listening exercises on an individual basis. Second, the course replaced pattern drills with exercises called manipulations. Although repetition drills were removed, some substitution drills were still found in the books. The majority of these manipulations were open questions that made students think and come up with creative answers. This course was definitely the beginnings of the communicative approach to the teaching of Spanish at DLI, and became a model for other DLI courses. Besides the cassette recorder, there were no technological breakthroughs in the 1970s and 80s. The cassette lab replaced the reel-to-reel lab, with a recorder installed in each student station. At this time, being able to play tapes at their own pace, students could do transcription and gisting (summarizing) exercises in the lab. Later on came the stand-alone computer lab, which used some commercial software and DLI developed programs. Unfortunately, many of these programs contained countless fill-in, multiple choice, and mechanical exercises. At the beginning these labs were not networked, providing only materials contained in each computer's hard drive or from CD's, many of them developed in house. Early on and again, at the urging of the users, this course was supplemented with Military Activities Modules (MAM), comparable to the BCEP exercises of the older course. However, all students, regardless of assignment, were exposed to MAM.

If you came in the late 1990s, you were exposed to the present Spanish course. Developed with the use of computers and in close proximity and coordination with the Spanish teachers and administrators, this course is a success story in its development and implementation. It was a contrast to the previous course, which was developed quite in isolation from the users. This new course is based heavily on "authentic materials" (printed, audio and video) with the appropriate copyright permissions. The course is indeed communicative, in that it uses authentic input to engage the student in real life communication. It is proficiency oriented in that it prepares the students according to the hierarchy of tasks expressed in the ILR proficiency descriptions. And it is in accord with the move toward the development of "performance objectives". Proficiency and performance skills are integrated throughout the course so that students progressively attain the desired level or skill. In the last several years three technological advances have modernized the teaching of Spanish. The first one was the introduction of the Multi-Media labs. The European and Latin American School (ELA) was the first DLI School to be assigned two of those labs. The second was the introduction of MP3 players, thus putting an end to the use of cassette tapes. The third was the installation of smart boards in each classroom. Every ELA classroom is now equipped with a Smart Board, through which all the text, audio, and video materials are delivered. A Smart Board is an interactive whiteboard that transforms the classroom into an interactive working and learning environment. With the combined power of a projector, computer and whiteboard, teachers can do everything they do on their computer – and more. Simply, they use their index finger as the mouse to touch the interactive whiteboard and highlight key points, access applications, web sites, TV cable programs, and are able to write (and erase) notes in electronic ink. Then, they save their work to files that that can be later reused, printed, e-mailed, or posted to a Web site.

These last three technological innovations emerged after the development of the current Spanish course. However, because the course is well organized, it was simple to convert all analog (text, audio, and video) materials into digital format, and fit them into a new system.

Since the 1960s the methodology has evolved and the technology has advanced. Thus, from audio-lingual to communicative, from overhead projectors to smart boards, from analog tape recorders to digital MP3 players, and from Reel-to-Reel labs to Multi-Media labs, the teaching of Spanish at DLI has indeed come a long way. ❖

Spanish department chairperson Dr. Jorge Kattan (2nd from right) and these four Spanish faculty: (L to R) Edward Moos, Enrique Berrios, Alida Stenenberg, and Juan Maguna, are some of the professionals who participated in the above described programs.

اللغة العربيّة

Arabic Basic Course
Transition from 47 to 63 weeks and from the "Abdelmalek" (audio-lingual) course to the "Gulf to the Ocean" (communicative) course.
DLIAA Newsletter VI - October 2006

In 1989 there were several evident challenges in the Middle East School (then only one school). For example, the Arabic curriculum, which had been developed in the early 1970s was in sorely need of revamping, and actually needed to be replaced. Also, the General Officer's Steering Committee (GOSC) had challenged the Institute to bring 80 percent of its graduates in all languages to the Listening 2, Reading 2 level (L2/R2) by FY93. Speaking was not yet included in that goal. Furthermore, after years of DLI lobbying, the GOSC had approved the extension of the Arabic Basic Course from 47 to 63 weeks to meet the 80 goal in Arabic. This article deals with the transition from the 47 to the 63 week Arabic course and the elimination of the locally brewed "Abdelmalek" (name of its author) course in favor of the commercial "From the Gulf to the Ocean" course, also known as the GO course, named for the geographical area from the Persian Gulf to the Atlantic Ocean.

Attempting to lengthen the duration of language courses at DLI is probable a 60 year old effort. It is believed that back in 1946-47, a maximum of 47 weeks was decided for the more difficult courses considering that the military services could not afford to have a serviceperson more than one year (52 weeks) away from mission duties. Within those 52 weeks there would be a two-week December holiday break, another one-week break in the middle of the course, and another week or two lost in holidays, for a total of 5 weeks of down time. Although there was always talk about making those courses longer, the 47-week maximum held up until the late 1980s.

Then, in 1989 the GOSC challenged the institute to bring 80 percent of its graduates in all languages to the L2/R2 level by FY 1993, and approved the extension of the Arabic basic course to meet this goal. Also in 1989 a new management team took the reins of the Middle East School. Under this new leadership the Arabic departments would eliminate the 16-week dialect extension (add on) courses. This new 63-week course, then divided into four terms (not semesters), would for the first time integrate the commercial GO course and the much revised DLI developed Abddelmalek (AM) course in the first term; that is, in the first 21 weeks. Term II would consist of more Abddelmalek and GO-type modules developed locally. Dialect "flavor" and Final Learning Objectives training would be integrated into terms III and IV; that is, in the last 24 weeks.

The Arabic 47-week course was chosen for extension because of the difficulty and complexity of the Modem Standard Arabic/Dialect combination and the traditionally low performance of Arabic language students on the Defense Language Proficiency Test (DLPT). As a matter of record, the percentage of DLI students meeting the L2/R2 DLI goal with the 47-week program and DLPT III had been a sluggish 20 percent in fiscal years 1987, 88 and 89.

Before the extension to 63 weeks, most Arabic students finished the 47-week basic course and then continued on with one of three 16-week dialect courses (Egyptian, Syrian, and Gulf), meaning that they studied Arabic for a total of 63 weeks, already a record length for a basic course at DLI. The first classes entered training under this new 63-week concept in the fall of 1989.

Arabic 47 Week Course (1972-1989)	Dialect Add on		
Abdelmalek Course (Audio Lingual) (47 wks)	(Egyptian, Syrian, and Gulf Dialects) (16 weeks)		
Arabic 63 Week Course (1990-1993)			
Term I (21 ks)	Term II (18 wks)	Term III (12 wks)	Term IV (12 wks)
AM & GO type matls	AM & GO type materials	FLO's Dialect Flavor	FLO's Dialect Flavor

This new 63-week paradigm brought big challenges. The emphasis on heavy doses of Modern Standard Arabic (MSA) throughout the 63 weeks in fact eliminated the structured 16-week dialect courses, per se, creating a materials void that had to be filled immediately without course development assets for such effort. Brain storming sessions with department chairs and teams leaders led to the conclusion that each team would have to extract authentic materials from newspapers, magazines, and recorded audio and video sources, then develop FLO type exercises, with questions and exercises based on those materials to be presented to the students as soon as they were developed. Instructors began to produce an avalanche of supplementary materials. They were instructed not to be concerned with copy machines allotted numbers of copies and do what was necessary to accomplish the job of delivering the materials in a timely manner. The fact that almost every instructor created his or her own materials gave the faculty such motivational boost, that many of them put their exercises in binders and had them printed at the Printing Plant. Fortunately, copyright releases existed for all the sources used. In those years, the Arabic script was once again allowed to be taught, after the Standard Arabic Transliteration Training System (SATTS) had been dropped in 1984. When the National Security Agency (NSA) revived its call for job specific training for cryptological students, called Final Learning Objectives (FLOs), the Arabic departments formed a team of civilian and military language instructors to develop a set of materials for the final term of the course, including the reintroduction of SATTS. Work also began in the Testing Division on a new Arabic DLPT IV.

Before the extension to 63 weeks, changes made in early 1989 to the 47-week program already saw a healthy increase from 20 percent to 31 percent L2/R2 in FY90, with only a one percent increase in academic attrition. Lengthening the course to 63 weeks meant further changes to the program. For example, in the first two terms, the traditional Abdelmalek course, developed at DLI, grammatically organized, and audio-lingual in methodology, was combined with the GO course, commercially developed, functionally organized and proficiency oriented in methodology. This combination enhanced learning from two directions. On the one hand, language was thrown at the students in sizable chunks, forcing them to derive global meaning. On the other hand, smaller portions of language were presented sequentially and systematically. These seemingly unlike approaches were successfully melded, greatly benefiting the Cryptological Training System (CTS) and non-CTS students. Students also benefited from the great variety of authentic materials added by the teachers.

The Abdelmalek course was traditional, grammar-based, and audio-lingual in methodology. It was written under contract in 1972-73 by Dr. Zaki Abdelmalek, a professor on leave from Utah State University, who worked with a group of DLI Arabic instructors and developed the 47-week long course in the record time of one year. NSA had heavy input throughout its development, as it was geared primarily for the listening skill and for students of the Cryptological Training System. During the mid 1980s, efforts were made to adapt the Abdelmalek course to the communicative approach, and as proficiency scores showed at the time, it was not successful across the board.

"The Abdelmalek curriculum had been developed by DLI in the early seventies. It presented second language learning primarily as a process of building proficiency through the practice of discrete elements of the target language, especially at the phonetic, morphological, semantic and syntactic levels. Contextualization of these language segments was limited. For the most part, the necessary practice was accomplished thru drill – that is, a pattern was presented by the teacher or text, and students manipulated that pattern to try to match a predetermined outcome. The materials reflected, therefore, an audio-lingual approach. However, insofar as grammar rules were frequently presented at the outset of drill work and not necessarily at its conclusion (where the more inductive audio-lingual approach would have them), the Abdelmalek curriculum also encompassed a grammar/translation approach to language teaching. The heavy use or translation drills also derived from that method, being generally eschewed by audio linguists. With some noteworthy exceptions, these two methods dominated task definition in the traditional curriculum."

The GO, a commercial course, was basically introduced as a proficiency oriented package. It was developed by Lebanese lin-

---

* See Molly Lewis Hulse, A Comparison of the GO and AM Curriculum in the *Teaching of Arabic as a Second Language at the DLI*, A Classroom ethnography (MIIS. 1988).

guists in the late 70s and published in France for the first time in 1979. In the mid-80s, the Middle East School adapted it to laserdisc technology and also developed materials following its format and methodology. These DLI created GO-type materials were developed in the late 80s to complement the topical and functional domains of the commercial curriculum. Although similar in format and methodology to the commercial course, the laserdisc component was not continued in these materials due to the conflicting priorities of also developing terms II and IV to extend the course from 47 to 63 weeks.

"The GO curriculum, as translated by a DLI development team from its traditional text and film strip format into interactive video software, worked from the premise that language learning proceeds from the general to the specific. That is, discourse-level, natural chunks of language are the matrix from which students tease out the pattern and meaning of more discrete elements of the text, whether at the syntactic, semantic of morphological level. While their initial comprehension of such a text may be far from complete, students take from this first exposure a context within which subsequent interactions with the teacher take form. The teacher's role in this curriculum, according to DLI curriculum designers, is to move the students from a general understanding of a chunk of discourse to a more complete understanding of its constituent elements, within the context established by the original text."**

As we see, the combination of the GO and Abdelmalek methodologies proved appropriate for course objectives during the transition period, as shown by results of proficiency scores and students performance in follow-on training. The first classes taking the 63-week course graduated in early 1991 with exceptionally high scores. More than 75 percent of the students in the first three classes scored at the L2/R2 level or higher.

Surprisingly, this unlikely mix of commercial and DLI-made materials worked relatively well in this time of transition. As mentioned above, the GO text materials came supplemented with antiquated film strip technology synchronized with audio cassette tapes. Fortunately, the recordings had been made by professional actors, who used their skills to put emotion, sarcasm, joy, surprise, into their voices to fit the different situations. So, when the Middle

---

** Ibid

East School decided to transfer this old technology into laserdisc, the results were amazing. The cartoon type filmstrip would come to life in the computer screen when the actors voices were superimposed, creating semi-real dialogue exchanges. Thus, each lesson was introduced using these devices. When the entire commercial course was transferred to laserdiscs in 1989, the Arabic departments became the first departments at the institute to begin using stand-alone computers with laserdisc technology in regular classrooms.

An Arabic Curriculum Review (ACR) held in May 1991 and headed by Peter Molan of NSA recommended retiring the Abdelmalek course. Accordingly, beginning in 1992, the Arabic program began reducing the number of Abdelmalek hours and increasing the number of From the Gulf to the Ocean hours. By mid-1993, the Abdelmalek course had been eliminated. The commercial course stood alone in terms I and II, followed by dialect flavor and Final Learning Objectives training in terms III and IV.

Fully 60 percent of the students graduating in FY 1992 reached L2/R2/S1, as speaking had now been added to the goal. When the Board of Visitors toured in September they singled out the school for praise, lauding the "impressive success in the increased proficiency level of Arabic language students as a result of extending the course to 63 weeks." When the percentage of students meeting the goal was calculated using the more recent L2/R2/S2 goal, Arabic had achieved 46 percent in FY92 and 44 percent in FY 1993. This small decline, however, was influenced by an all-time low 3 percent academic attrition rate, less than half the previous year.

The success of the Arabic program extension ensured the extension to 63 weeks of the Chinese, Japanese and Korean programs.

Arabic 63-week program proves successful.

DLI *GLOBE* – March 1991

What do Robert Boctor, Mounir Safwany, Aida Hallaq, Samir Nimri, Samir Rizkallah, Mourice Said and Shawky Zeidan have in common? These seven Arabic instructors pioneered the first 63-week Arabic program from beginning to end. They are primarily responsible for the high performance of the 28 graduates, 79 percent of whom met the proficiency-level two goal in listening and reading -with 57 percent of them scoring level two in all three skills. These teachers' efforts to train the students to the highest levels motivated their charges, in turn. Students maintained extremely high morale, even though their staying in school during the Christmas holidays.

On Feb. 7, three weeks ahead of their original graduation date, the Middle East School held a graduation ceremony for the students, whose holiday leave had been canceled due to *Operation Desert Shield.*

The history of the 63-week course began recently. In June 1989 the General Officer Steering Committee authorized the Defense Language Institute to extend the Arabic Basic Course, a category IV language, from 47 to 63 weeks to reach the Proficiency Enhancement Program objectives that, by 1993, call for 80 percent of DLI's students to achieve level two in listening and in one other skill.

The Arabic course was chosen for extension because of the difficulty and complexity of the Modern Standard Arabic/dialect combination and the traditionally low performance of Arabic language students on the Defense Language Proficiency Test. As a matter of record, the percentage of DLI students meeting the DLI goal with the 47-wek program and the DLPT III had been a sluggish 20 percent in fiscal years 1987, 1988 and 1999.

Changes made in early 1989 to the 47-week program saw a healthy increase to 31 percent in FY90, with only a one percent increase in academic attrition. Lengthening the course to 63 weeks brought further changes in the curriculum. For example, in the first two terms, the traditional *Abdelmalek* course, developed at DLI, grammatically organized, and audio-lingual in methodology, was combined with the *Gulf to the Ocean* course, commercially developed, functionally organized, and proficiency oriented in methodology. This combination has enhanced learning from two directions. On the one hand, language is thrown at the students in sizable chunks, forcing them to derive global meaning. On the other hand, smaller portions of language are presented sequentially and systematically. These seemingly unlikely approaches have been successfully melded, greatly benefitting signal and human intelligence students, who have also benefited from the great variety of authentic materials added by the teachers.

Early in 1990 several teachers were assigned to specifically develop *Authentic Arabic Interactive materials* (AAIM) in listening, reading and speaking to be used in Terms III and IV. The dialect phase begins as students enter Term III (at about the 37th week). It consists of two hours daily of Egyptian, Syrian or Iraqi *dialect*–depending on the initial assignment of the students.

Parallel to the dialect training, the MSA curriculum continues four hours a day with emphasis on Final Learning Objectives plus DLI and commercially developed exercises based on authentic materials such as "*A Week in the Middle East*" (WME), an English package of newspaper articles covering 20 distinct topics. The course ends with heavy doses of reading and listening with authentic materials.

The success of the Arabic program almost ensures an extension to 63 weeks to the Chinese, Japanese and Korean programs.❖

History of the Serbian/Croatian program at DLIFLC (1948 to 1998)
DLI *GLOBE* - November 1997

The American Heritage Dictionary defines Serbo-Croatian as "the Slavic language of the Serbs and the Croats". In this article I will refer to Serbo-Croatian as both the language department and the language program at the Defense Language Institute Foreign Language Center (DLIFLC) and its predecessors from 1948 to 1989. However, the language branch and program from 1993 to the 1998 will be referred to as Serbian/Croatian, a change made by DLIFLC to better reflect the political situation and the fact that in academic circles Serbian and Croatian are more and more considered two separate variants of one language, with tendencies to become two different languages. Serbian is written using the Cyrillic alphabet, Croatian uses the Latin alphabet.

In 1948, the Army Language School created the Serbo-Croatian department alongside several other Slavic language departments. Their students lived in wooden barracks (demolished in the early 70s) located in what is now Soldier's field, while language instruction was delivered in the buildings to the north and south of the field. From that time and until it was discontinued in 1989 along with nine other low density language programs, the department taught a 47-week basic course that included exclusively the Serbian variant, except for the last several weeks which were reserved for the Croatian variant. The department remained relatively stable from the late 1940's to the middle 1980's, consisting of a chairperson, a secretary, and some seven to ten teachers.

From the beginning of its history, the department was under the same administrative umbrella with Russian and other East European languages. That umbrella organization changed its name from Slavic Group to Slavic School in 1984, then to East European School, then back to Slavic School and finally was referred to as Central European School from 1989 to 1993. In 1988 -- in the first reorganization of its kind -- the Institute moved to combine several declining language programs into one Multi-Language department. Thus, the East European School brought together the Bulgarian, Greek, Hungarian, and Serbo-Croatian programs, named them branches, and put them under a newly organized Multi-Language department. The future of these programs had begun to look grim in 1987 when the Institute began shifting toward contracting out course development. That year, plans were laid out to contract out course development of the Greek, Hungarian, Persian, and Serbo-Croatian basic courses.

By early 1989, the interest of intelligence collection in certain East European countries was almost non-existent. As a result, the influx of students in those languages was at such low levels the Institute seized the opportunity to realize savings by contracting them out. Thus, after a Commercial Activities A76 study, the teaching of Serbo-Croatian at the Defense Language Institute was discontinued in late 1989. Any subsequent requirements for training were filled through the Foreign Service Institute or through contractors hired by the DLI Washington Office. However, by 1992 the principal user agencies were already predicting increasing demands for certain languages in the Balkan region, including the need for military linguists proficient in Serbo-Croatian.

The United States involvement in Bosnia-Herzegovina produced a renewed interest in the languages of the region. As a result, in December 1992 under the auspices of the Central European School, a Serbian/Croatian effort began to evolve with the hiring of a former retired DLI instructor to prepare a Serbian/Croatian Military Survival Kit and to develop the "cross-training" (or conversion) concept. The idea was that students who already knew a language closely related to Serbian/Croatian, such as Czech, Polish, or Russian, could learn it in about one fourth of the time as someone beginning from scratch. In early 1993, this instructor and another one borrowed from the Russian program began teaching the first 15-week cross-training course to six resident Air Force and Army students. They also began teaching six students from Fort Meade, MD, and Fort Bragg, NC, via Video Tele-training (VTT). The resident students were physically located in the same room with the instructors and concurrently received the same training as the distant learning students. This may be the only resident/VTT combination effort ever accomplished at the Institute. In the spring of 1993, the Fort Ord Contracting Office hired four contract instructors for a period of 90-120 days to assist in developing and teaching the first 12-week resident conversion course for students proficient in Russian, Polish, or Czech. The program also included refresher training for a number of native and semi-native speakers of Serbian/Croatian. Once the program was established, a civilian and a military instructor went to Royal Air Force Mildenhall, England, to cross-train 15 Russian linguists.

In October 1993, when the Central European School was disbanded, the Czech, Slovak, and Serbian/Croatian programs were reassigned to the Multi-Language department of the newly formed East European School II (EE2), located in Nicholson Hall. By that time, the contract instruction had ended and the conversion effort continued with temporary instructors hired by DLIFLC. During the first quarter of FY94, 60 former Russian and Czech students reported to EE2 to take the conversion course, now 16 weeks in length. Most graduates went on to perform duties in the Bosnian region. In 1994 a three-month Mobile Training Team (MTT) consisting of two instructors provided enhancement training to 19 students in Fort Richardson, Alaska and another MTT of one civilian and one military instructor traveled to Chicksands, England to train 10 students preparing to deploy to the Bosnian theater. From February to June 1995, yet another MTT of two instructors was sent to Rota, Spain to provide enhancement training to 10 Navy students. While in EE2, the branch began plans for the development of the basic course as the further refinement of the conversion course continued. The basic course combined all existing materials (commercial and otherwise), while the conversion course materials were developed from existing sources and newly created materials, The branch built the basic course using materials (modules) given to the Institute as a courtesy of the Canadian government, the existing Foreign Service Institute course, the commercial and primary college-level textbook written by Thomas Magner, and the materials already used in the conversion course.

In November 1993, the Testing Division began the design and development of the Serbian/Croatian Defense Language Proficiency Test (DLPT) IV battery. This would be the first and only DLPT to contain separate listening and reading portions for two language variants. In the reading portion Croatian was in the Latin alphabet, Serbian in Cyrillic. The Serbian/Croatian DLPT IV was completed in June 1995.

In May 1995, the Czech and Serbian/Croatian programs moved again, this time to join the Polish, Ukrainian, and Byelorussian programs in the Multi-Language department of the now called European School I (E1), located near Soldier's Field. This move returned the Serbian/Croatian program to the same geographical area it occupied in the late 1940's. Before the program moved however, the input of conversion students decreased and several instructors were laid off. In E1, the branch continued planning for the first 47 week basic course class scheduled to begin in June 1996. A dearth of course materials compelled decision makers in E1 and the Curriculum Division to select the Canadian modules as the foundation of the basic course. The Canadian materials were basically Serbian oriented and sometimes used the Latin alphabet to represent the Serbian variant. An effort began in February 1996 to develop corresponding Croatian materials and to replace the Latinized Serbian with Cyrillic. The Croatian development effort ended in March 1997. The Canadian modules were not a finished product. The materials arrived only in printed form and were difficult to revise without completely re-entering the corrected portions into a word processing format in a computer. Furthermore, the quality of the printing made scanning a time consuming chore.

In June 1996, thirty students reported for the basic course. Meanwhile the conversion effort continued in resident mode and branch instructors continued providing VTT to students in the field. There was another requirements surge in early 1997. Three contract courses were established to fulfill this need. One course for 40 students was conducted in Monterey by four contract instructors hired by the DLIFLC Washington Office. The other two courses were conducted in Fort Hood, Texas (Nov 96 and Feb 97) via MTT with one contract instructor, and one DLIFLC instructor on a rotating basis. Furthermore, the DLIFLC Washington Office organized four contract courses on the East Coast from Jan 96 to Jun 97. A comparison of the conversion courses conducted in Washington, D.C., Fort Hood, and DLIFLC showed that students trained in the DLIFLC environment obtained higher proficiency levels in the three tested skills of listening, reading and speaking.

During 1997, E1 continued adjusting the conversion course from information received in sensing sessions and applying all lessons learned to the basic course.

In June 1997, the first basic course students since 1989 graduated with zero academic attrition. However, the percentage of L2-R2-S2 (26 percent) was disappointingly low. It became obvious the instructors had not successfully transitioned from teaching the conversion course to mature, experienced language students; to teaching the new and untried basic course to young, inexperienced language students. The basic course materials and the tests were still in the process of being validated, thus the instructors did not have the bench marks they needed to accurately assess the progress of their students. As a result, eight of the graduates (who in any other language program would have been dropped) could not be waived to follow-on training. In an unprecedented move, the Army and Air Force commanders met with representatives of the Office of Plans and Programs, the Provost Office, and European School I and agreed to 12 more weeks of additional instruction for those students.

September 1997 brought good news to the Serbian/Croatian branch. Seventy-nine percent of the conversion class students graduating that month received level-two or higher in listening (L), reading (R), and speaking (S). These were the highest scores ever recorded for a conversion class. The second basic course class graduated 9 students with zero academic attrition. Six of these students (67 percent) achieved or surpassed the DLIFLC goal of L2-R2-S2. One of the students reached level 3 in the three skills. The 12-week enhancement training for the eight students remaining from the first basic course also ended in September. All the students but one increased their score by at least a half-level in both listening and reading (speaking was not retested), and one increased listening by

1½ levels. The proficiency scores of conversion and basic course students from FY93 to FY96 can be seen in the following charts.

CONVERSION COURSE STUDENTS

	FY93	FY94	FY95	FY96	FY97
Academic Attrition	0%	0%	0%	0%	0%
Graduates	62	77	13	54	48
Number of level 2-2-2	4	8	3	26	20
Percentage of level 2-2-2	6%	10%	23%	48%	42%
Average DLAB	109	112	117	106	101

BASIC COURSE STUDENTS

				FY96	FY97
Academic Attrition				0%	0%
Graduates				27	9
Number of level 2-2-2				7	6
Percentage of level 2-2-2				26%	67%
Average DLAB				106	116

The accomplishments of this small program from 1993 to 1997 had been surprisingly good given the limitations of course materials, inexperienced teachers, and personnel turbulence. With no academic attrition for five years and a steady increase in proficiency results since 1993, the Serbian/Croatian branch faculty had proudly established itself with the mainstream of the Institute.

On 1 October 1997, the Serbian/Croatian program underwent yet another reorganization. The Multi-Language department, with the Polish and Czech programs, moved to the European and Latin American School. Serbian/Croatian remained in E1, thus becoming a department in its own right, with an expected increase in student input during the next several years. The department was then composed of a chairperson, a secretary, plus 14 civilian and 2 military instructors. It had 75 basic students, but no conversion course students. The Serbian/Croatian department was located in buildings 205 and 206 in the lower part of the institute, near the Post Theater. On 9 October 1997 the department was ready to receive 30 basic students and the next conversion class of 10 students was to arrive in July of 1998.

Graduates of our Serbian/Croatian program could proudly claim they learned and were tested in two language variants. They could even claim in some circles they learned two languages. In Churchillian parlance one can say that "never before in the history of language training had the U.S. government produced *"TWO FOR THE PRICE OF ONE."*

Haitian Coat of Arms

Haitian Creole Project
A Real Team Effort
DLI *GLOBE* - February 1995

Note: In Sept. 1994, President Clinton ordered 20,000 troops to Haiti to force the departure of military rulers led by General Cedras. This act led to the return of elected President Jean-Bertrand Aristide and restored democracy in Haiti.

The warning order came in late October 1994. The Department of the Army sent a message to DLI indicating that Haitian Creole linguists might be needed as early as the first week of December.

The exact number of linguists required was unknown at the time. It could be 120 students in a single bunch, or 600 in staggered groups. French linguists would have to cross-train in Haitian Creole in a course lasting 10 to 12 weeks. The entrance requirement for the cross training would be a current 2-2-2 in French.

Despite the uncertainty, DLI had to plan for the training. Dr. Ray Clifford, DLI Provost, determined that the training would take place in East European School II (EE2) and consequently summoned Ben De La Selva, EE2's dean, to his office. The school had extra space for classrooms and offices, and across the street, Foxtrot Company would house the students.

Clifford and De La Selva agreed to reassign Ani Frazier from Information Management to EE2 as project officer for the effort. At the same time, word came that a current Thai student, SSG Cassandra Woel, reared and educated in Haiti, claimed native proficiency in Creole as well as professional proficiency in French. Woel was also familiar with DLI curricula, as she had attended the DLI Russian Basic and Le Fox courses in the 1980s. MAJ David Tatman, associate dean of Asian School I, instructed Woel to report to EE2 after 3 p.m. every day to support the Haitian Creole effort.

Frazier and Woel immediately inventoried DLI's holdings and examined the few existing texts, including a 1975 DLI course developed by Mrs. Rolande Tournier in consultation with Dr. Albert Valdman of Indiana University. In coordination with Christa Rutsche of the Curriculum Division and Les Turpin of Production Coordination, several adjunct texts and dictionaries were ordered.

Tournier's Haitian Creole project, an entirely audio-lingual effort, was apparently terminated in the mid-70s during the validation stage. Consequently, the camera-ready copy contained numerous blue-pencil corrections in the margins. Also, it was entirely typewritten using a now-obsolete orthographic system. Frazier and Woel's challenge was to convert this old course into a modern edition by making all the corrections, including using the newest Creole transcription system.

At this point, Pavel Bielecki, a Czech instructor with computer expertise, and Peter Schultz, EE2's Information Management officer, started scanning the Tournier materials and converting them into computer files. Frazier then compared the old and new texts, fine-tuned the format, and passed the materials on to Woel, who reviewed and corrected the Creole and modernized the orthography.

The Christmas break, in some ways, separated the team members and threatened to slow down the gathered momentum. Frazier and Schultz continued to work, but due to family problems Woel and Bielecki had to take leave. Through the efforts of MAJ Kirt Quist, EE2's associate dean, Canada-based Woel was able to communicate with the team via Lingnet, a DLI electronic bulletin board. Frazier and Schultz sent Creole lessons to Woel in Canada, and Woel reviewed, revised and corrected them, then sent them back to DLI, all via Lingnet.

While the development efforts were going on, a team of two faculty trainers, Solfrid Johansen and SSG Donny Weber, went to Washington, D.C. to present the Instructor Certification Course, ICC, to seven Haitian teachers who had been hired through contract by the DLI Washington office. Johansen and Weber carried with them the first five lessons of the revised Tournier course.

In the meantime, Quist took advantage of the holiday break to coordinate numbers, faces, and spaces. The students--now numbering 34 and all from the Army--would be housed in E and F companies. The teachers, now numbering seven, would be billeted in the Sun Bay apartments at the Presidio of Monterey Annex (formerly Fort Ord) and they would have access to three rental cars. Quist identified ten rooms for classrooms and offices in Building 848, the home of EE2.

Haitian Creole is considered a separate language and, although very different from French, learning it can be partially facilitated by a good grasp of the latter. According to authorities, "*French Creole is best viewed as a language derived from two basically Romance types of speech -- French and Afro-Portuguese Pidgin (APP), a contact language.-- APP developed along the coast of Africa during the slave trade "exhibiting Romance grammatical features, a mixture of some African features and a vocabulary derived from a variety of sources, but with a preponderance of forms from Portuguese and other Romance languages,*" according to an Indiana University Publications book, "Basic Course in Haitian Creole," by Dr. Albert Valdman.

During the first week of January, final word from the Department of the Army confirmed the need for the linguists, so final plans for the course could move forward and the course could begin.

Seven teachers, Gina Almonte, Jean Raymond Anglade, Guylene Desir, Faustin Evans, Patrique Francisque, Fenol Jean, and Suzy LeMaire arrived on Monday, Jan 16, 1995. However, by the end of that week, only eighteen of the students had arrived. While the teachers continued their faculty training, Mr. Rene de Barros from Technology Integration gave the students refresher training in

French. Plans were finalized for the program to officially begin on Thursday, January 26, 1995 when all students would have arrived.

Thus, three months of timely coordination by a host of DLI faculty and staff members ensured that an old, typed, audio-lingual course, modernized and revised using state of the art electronic technology, was properly delivered by contract instructors to service members ready to deploy to Haiti.

As was the case with other hot spots in the world such as Granada, Saudi Arabia, and Somalia, this team effort once again illustrates that DLI can act quickly and effectively in producing materials and linguists on short notice. Indeed a real team effort.

One Day in the Life of John Smith (aka Ivan Denisovich Kuznetsov)
A brief account of DLI's Russian program since the 1970s
Printed with permission from Dr. Luba Grant*

Acknowledgement: My special thanks to former students Neil Granoien (current DLI Vice Chancellor) and Joe Krupski (DLI Chairperson - retired) for sharing their memories with me. I'm also especially grateful to my colleagues Alex Vorobiov, Richard Donovan, and Robert Love for proofreading the article and providing valuable input.

"Ne strelyajte! Eto ya, a ne utka!" (Don't shoot! It's me…not a duck!) -- This was my introduction to teaching the Russian Basic Course in the early 1970s. Upon arrival at the Defense Language Institute (DLI) straight from the university - where those students learned Russian at a leisurely pace from selected commercial textbooks by practicing myriads of declensions and conjugations and diligently translating into English Pushkin's *Eugene Onegin,* or depending on the teacher, Lermontov's *A Hero of Our Time,* and taking courses in Old Church Slavonic -- I was struck by the scope, pace, and organization of the Russian Basic Course (RBC) at DLI.

The daily learning activities of a student studying Russian in those days were quite predictable. Every single lesson of the Russian course (and other language courses) had been developed around a lengthy dialog (up to five pages long) that the students had to memorize and recite start to finish every third day (I'll bet some of you still remember famous lines from your days here at DLI, such as those above). So, in those days, if at 8 o'clock in the morning you'd have gone from section to section of the same class, you'd have heard the same questions and the same responses from the pairs of students whose turn it was to recite the dialog. (By the way, each student was given a full Russian name, including patronymic, right from the start of the course. Thus, a typical Russian student's name appears in the title above, based on A. Solzhenitsyn's *One Day in the Life of Ivan Denisovich*.) Was that the most exciting part of the day? From the teacher's point of view, you can bet it wasn't! I don't think most of the students found this lesson to be very exciting either. As the two students were taking their turn reciting the dialog, the rest were probably peacefully dozing off as often as they could.

The dialog was always followed by numerous pattern transformations and substitution drills, as well as dialog recombination practiced either in class or in the language lab. "Listen and repeat," was probably the most frequent order given in the classroom and in the lab at that time. And the translations! Don't forget those! The students translated long sentences into Russian as part of their homework, and new sentences (often made up by the teacher to illustrate intricate grammatical points) would be translated in class, where one student would write the translation on the board while others wrote in their notebooks. The class would carefully analyze the mistakes prior to proceeding to a new sentence. The entire cycle of the lesson -- dialog preparation, dialog recitation, pattern drills, translation -- would be repeated every third day. And so on, and so forth. For 47 weeks.

Sounds boring?, maybe. But the course also had many reading and conversation hours. In the 1960s reading and the follow-up discussions were important parts of the course. *Dva Kapitana* and *A Hero of Our Time* were read by the students with great interest. Conversations were carried out in class on numerous topics, and many former students fondly recall the stories their teachers told them about their interesting lives prior to their arrival to US. Students were expected to speak only Russian all the time. Emphasis on proper pronunciation and intonation was very strong. The faculty and students were able to create an immersion environment that was conducive to language learning and acquiring knowledge about the culture and customs of the country through many out-of-class activities, such as picnics, trips to San Francisco, and famous choirs. Until very recently (yes, we're getting old) university Slavic departments all over the country often had at least one Russian professor from this generation of students who got his/her first Russian -- and fell in love with it – at DLI. Furthermore, some of the students later returned to work at DLI as instructors, chairpersons, deans, and even a vice chancellor.

The Russian Basic Course used in the early 1970s was based on the Basic Course developed about a decade earlier by DLI teachers under the guidance of Anatoly Flaume. It consisted of 150+ lessons, but in the 70s only about 120 lessons were taught during the 47 weeks of instruction. The course was divided into two tracks. One was the Army track, which was the original version of the course, with gray covers -- all students would begin with those. The other was the Russian Basic Aural Comprehension Course, which was a new version with blue books, developed later by a different team. That track was used by Air Force, Navy, and Marine students in the second half of the course. The original course, in addition to teaching the language, introduced students to the geography of the Soviet Union and a detailed version of the origins and history of Russia, covering, rather extensively for a basic course, the main Russian tsars and major events in pre-revolutionary Russia, then ending with the October Revolution and a brief overview of post-revolutionary Russia. "Govorite tol'ko po-russki!" (Speak Russian only!) was a phrase frequently heard by the students at that time.

The Russian Basic Aural Comprehension Course (blue covers) greatly reduced the area-studies component of the original RBC and put more emphasis on job-specific objectives: transcription; number dictations; and numbers in context. Students taking this portion of the course could be observed in the lab listening to "real" communication between two or more military personnel. "Hawk, Hawk! This is Eagle. Over!" sounded quite realistic, even though the scenarios were written and recorded by DLI faculty.
In the last part of the course all students would be divided into separate groups in order to give them a strong dose of service-

specific military terminology before sending them off to their next assignment. Thus, Army students would be taught, often by civilian faculty, the Russian words for trajectories, munitions, track vehicles, and many other military terms that remained mysterious to the faculty and the students alike. Air Force students could translate perfectly from one language to another communications during aircraft take-offs and landings, and many of the students told me later how, during commercial flights in the US, they would listen to the pilot's transmission in English and translate it into Russian in their head while waiting for a take-off or landing. Navy and Marine students built an extensive vocabulary of different types of ships and underwater munitions while learning Russian.

In 1974 - 1975 the two aforementioned programs were replaced by a course that was based on a different approach to language teaching, the delayed-speech approach. This course was developed under the leadership of Valerian Postovsky. The students taking this course were not required to practice speaking at the beginning of the program. Instead, they were exposed to a series of different picture frames, while listening to Russian, and would mark the correct responses on their answer sheets. Speaking would be introduced later in the course with the belief, that, due to their earlier exposure to the language, the students would be able to pick up this skill faster.

At the beginning of the 1980s a new Russian Basic Course was written by DLI's Course Development Division Russian branch, headed by Alex Vorobiov. This course eliminated the memorization of long dialogs, substantially modernized the area-studies component of the program, and stressed practice in job-related skills.

Beginning in the late 1980s and continuing into the 1990s, foreign-language teaching took a turn towards communicative, proficiency-oriented teaching. For this purpose, yet another RBC was written. This time an "in-house" approach was taken with another course developed by Russian School instructors, headed by George Rubinstein. The course was thematically organized and presented grammar and vocabulary in context. Each lesson had a discourse portion based on the then-current situation in the Soviet Union, around which numerous activities, integrating all three skills -- listening, reading, and speaking -- were built. Like the previous course of the early '80s, this course avoided dialog memorization and encouraged real-life communication. The sudden collapse of the Soviet Union made the area studies component of this course prematurely obsolete, but the core of the program continues to be used by the Russian faculty until this day. Thanks to the latest technology, e.g., Internet access and Smart Boards (see newsletter #III, Issue 3-04- July 2004) and clearly defined Final Learning (Proficiency) and Performance (Job Related) Objectives, instructors can now supplement the course with current authentic materials, without waiting for back-issues of Russian newspapers to arrive at DLI. If you go from section to section today, instead of the meticulous repetition of prescribed materials, you'll often see the students working in small groups on real-life tasks that address student learning needs. Since the outcome of the interaction often depends on student input, these days it is very difficult to guess what the consequences of such conversation will be. Indeed, a day in the life of student Ivan Denisovich Kuznetsov is no longer as predictable as it was in the '60s and '70s. There were other, less widely used Russian courses or portions of courses at DLI: the Basic Course Enrichment Program (BCEP) was one. This course mainly emphasized job-related skills for students going to Goodfellow Air Force Base. "Suggestopedia," also called the Lozanov method, was tried in the late '70s. In spite of the relaxed atmosphere of the course, soft lights, rocking armchairs, baroque music, and no homework, the experimental approach did not prove itself, and after just one iteration, all students returned to studying Russian the old-fashioned way. The Russian saying, "Povtoreniye -- mat' ucheniya" ("Repetition/Review is the mother of learning.") ruled once again. And instead of baroque music, Presidio of Monterey audiences would hear students enthusiastically singing popular Russian songs, such as *Katyusha, Podmoskovnye Vechera (Moscow Nights), and Dorogoy Dlinnoyu (Those Were the Days, My Friends)*. And even later, sometime in the 1980s, the Air Force decided to send its students to study Russian at DLI for only 37 weeks, instead of the programmed 47 weeks. This proved to be too short, so that still today the DLI Basic Course lasts for 47 weeks.

One major change that can be seen in the Russian program (and all programs here at DLI) is the way students are now tested. Needless to say, all students in the past were diligently graded by their teachers for about every activity in and outside the classroom: dialog recitation; class participation; homework; lab performance; effort; etc. And then there were endless tests...at the beginning, middle and end of the program. In addition to frequent vocabulary quizzes, larger tests were given every second week. The latter consisted mostly of translation from English into Russian and answering (in Russian) questions on area studies and history. Later times saw increased use of many true/false and multiple-choice tests. Then, of course, there was a grade for one's oral performance. Finally, all these grades were averaged together and that would be student's grade for the program.

Today DLI is accredited by the Accrediting Commission for Community and Junior Colleges of the Western Association of Schools and Colleges. Language programs are divided into semesters, with various course numbers following university patterns. All students earn college credits for their coursework at DLI. Each course is graded separately. But even more important is that prior to graduating from DLI, students are tested in listening, reading, and speaking skills by certified testers (who are not their own teachers) trained by the Testing and Evaluation Division. In addition to their program course grades, they receive language proficiency levels in these three skills which are based on the Interagency Skill Levels (Interagency Language Roundtable -- ILR) standards. (For a description of the various skill levels, see http://www.govtilr.org/.)

The size of the Russian program closely reflected the nature of the Cold War between the United States and the Soviet Union. At one time, the Russian program was so large that it required the creation of two off-site campuses -- one at Lackland Air Force Base, and another at the Presidio of San Francisco. At its peak, DLI's Russian program consisted of two-and-a-half Schools devoted to Russian language and area studies, with more than 200 Russian teachers and nearly 2000 Russian students. Today, since the fall of the Soviet Union, the program is significantly smaller and is combined into one school together with the Spanish program, once again, "down the hill," by the Post Theater. In spite of its small size, the Russian program retains its status and reputation for trying innovative approaches, and it is the first program at DLI to be making the full transition to the Proficiency Enhancement Program (PEP). The PEP program at DLI will attempt to bring 80 percent of students to higher proficiency levels (2+/2+/2) by reducing the section size from ten to six students for category III and IV languages and modernizing the curricula. It is anticipated that in the future, the PEP program, in addition to using a reduced class size, will also extend the course length by 12 weeks and require higher entry DLAB scores.

Much has changed since the early 1970s when I first began teaching at DLI, but throughout its history there have always been two constants. The first has been all the fine young men and women who have studied here in the past, are here now, and will be arriving here in the future. The second constant has been the teachers, whose dedication to their work and their commitment to their students has been ever present since the very beginning. Whether they were former immigrants who fled the Russian Revolution, escaped Russia during World War II, or came to the U.S. from China, or whether they came much later from the post-war USSR or today's Russian Federation and former Soviet republics – the majority of teachers is totally devoted to their profession and take pride in the accomplishments of their students. And the students are the Institute's reason for being. They and their teachers form a strong bond and together they are the source of all the memories and so many accomplishments. So if you happen to visit DLI in the near future, don't be surprised if a former teacher suddenly gives you a real bear hug and says, once again, "Govorite tol'ko po russki!", as if you had never left.

*Dr. Grant was the Dean of Russian Schools I and II from 1987 to 1993; Dean of Middle East School II (Arabic) from 1993 to 2002. Currently she is the Dean of Asian School I (Chinese, Japanese, Thai, and Tagalog). ❖

"Hauptmann Schnell Was Here"
A brief account of DLI's German program from the 1950s to now

DLIAA Newsletter II – April 2004
Printed with permission from Annette Scheibner*

Which German do early DLI graduates remember best? Erich Honeker, Helmut Schmidt, Helmut Kohl, Nena or even Boris Becker? Not at all – the answer has to be *Hauptmann Schnell*, his girlfriend Lilo and their Dackel Putzi. No idea who they are? Well, you must have graduated in the mid-eighties or later. You might remember Herrn Dübel, Herrn Böhler, Käte Biehl or even Frau Häusel. Or Katja Heinemann, Klaus-Otto Baumer, Angelika Wiechert and the Matters are still fresh in your mind. Who are these people, and how have they helped countless German Alumni master the challenge of learning German at DLI?

German was taught from the earliest days of DLI and is still taught today. Of course, after the fall of the wall, the program has shrunk from two departments to a small program of several teachers. The program now resides in Pomerene Hall (adjacent to the well-known Nisei Hall, the department's home during the 80s and early 90s).

After WWII, Dr. Münzer (you might remember Munzer Hall – the old library was named after him, unfortunately denying him his Umlaut) wrote the first set of textbooks, chronicling Hauptmann Schnell's adventures in Germany. It was a truly grammar-based program, teaching the exact same skill at the same time each day. Students had to memorize dialogues, practice grammar drills and follow Hauptmann Schnell for 92 Lessons. The students were separated into "speakers" and "listeners" and drilled accordingly.

The 80s brought the first major change with the in-house production of a trail-blazing communicative textbook. It contained 35 lessons and was lovingly referred to as the "Telefonbuch" due to its looks. Herr Dübel et al revolutionized teaching at DLI, and many other languages used the Telefonbuch as a prototype for their new textbooks. To complete the students' training, a commercial textbook named "Themen" was added, in which Katja and friends guided generations of DLI students through the higher roams of the German language and culture.

Today, DLI still uses Themen 1 & 2 in addition to a variety of materials and web-based exercises. We are fortunate to have the latest technology in our classrooms and labs, and with the help of the Multi-Media Lab, a smart board in every classroom, and the usual audio-visual equipment, we are able to bring Germany into the classroom in real life. Yet, one thing has not changed: students have to study hard, and practice, practice, practice...!

So if you ever see one of the old panels of the Berlin Wall and read "Hauptmann Schnell was here", you will now know who wrote it and why.

* Annette Scheibner is a German faculty member in the European and Latin American School. ❖

Dr Traian Ocneanu and Capt Alexander Burz, circa 1948

PERSONALITIES
Early Army Language School Pioneer Alexander "Alex" Burz Passes Away
DLI Newsletter VII - July 2005

About five years ago, Alex Burz, whom I had known since September 1972, gave me an old and yellow typewritten document that he had kept for over 50 years. It was Army Language School (ALS) General Order Number 8, dated 23 July 1948, which listed Dr. Traian Ocneanu and Captain Alexander Burz as Instructors of Romanian, effective July 1948. These two, and Dr. Adolph Mancil, formed part of the Romanian department in the Romanic-Scandinavian Languages division of the Army Language School. Alex, whose family had emigrated to the U.S. from Romania, was born in West Virginia in 1917. He had joined the Army during WWII and was an infantry major when he was discharged in 1944. His son Michael reports that during the 1940s Alex served in London, in the cabinet war rooms (Churchill War rooms).

In 1948 he was recalled to active duty as a captain on the recommendation of the Army Language School Commandant, and joined ALS first as a Romanian instructor, later becoming successively Romanian department chair, Romanic-Scandinavian Division Chief, and Assistant Director for Training. When in 1951 the military saw the need for French speaking officers in Indochina

(Vietnam), Alex was sent there, where he served as an aide and interpreter to General Thomas Trapnell, at that time Commander of the Military Assistance and Advisory Group (MAGG-Indochina). According to his son Michael, in 1954 and as part of his duties, Alex travelled briefly to Dien Bien Phu, only a few weeks before the French defeat.

Alex returned again to DLI in the late 60s as a French instructor (civilian). Ed Moos, a Navy French student in 1969, recalls Alex, now in his fifty's, as a tall, sharp, and elegant looking man and one of the best French instructors of the time. By 1972, when I first met him, he was back teaching Romanian. He had also become President of the Local Chapter of the National Federation of Federal Employees (NFFE) 1263. As such, he was an uncompromising fighter for instructors' working conditions, earning the respect of the faculty and the top military and civilian leadership. In the 1980s Alex again became Romanian department chair. At that time there were several small language departments, and Romanian instructors under his leadership were never more than a handful. In 1989 the inevitable happened when DLI decided to abolish several small programs. Thus, against his strong advice the Romanian department was abolished in 1989, together with the Serbian/Croatian, Albanian, Bulgarian, Indonesian, and Dari/ Pashto programs. Alex retired that same year.

In reality Alex never left DLI. His status as a former military officer allowed him access to the Institute's facilities even following the tighten security measures of post 9-11. Accordingly, he showed up at the Snack Bar on a daily basis and formed a "Stammtisch" (see photo on p. 29) with several old cronies and other retirees. More recently, Alex, who had been afflicted with diabetes in earlier years, suffered the greatest setback of his life. His left leg had to be amputated, leaving him without the ability to move around on his own. One complication followed another and as he was moved back and forth from the Monterey Convalescent Home to the Community Hospital, he saw his life slip away slowly until he passed away at the Monterey Convalescent Home on Monday, July 4th, 2005. ❖

Alfie Khalil signing Union Agreement with Col. Don Fischer

Alfie Tewfik Khalil
Union President (Feb 1947 - Nov 2006)
Taken from Memorial Program, 30 Nov 06.

Alfie Tewfick Khalil was born in El-Minia, Egypt, in 1947. Upon completion of high school he attended Cairo University and Ayin Shams University to study business commerce and economics. In 1969 he graduated with a Bachelor of Science degree in Business Administration.

After coming to the United States, Mr. Khalil continued his business education and studied economics at George Mason University in Virginia. He was employed as a substitute teacher in the Fairfax County Public School System, teaching Social Science and Government.

Mr. Khalil came to the Defense Language Institute Foreign Language Center (DLIFLC) as an Arabic language instructor in 1979. In 1989 he was elected union president of the American Federation of Government Employees, Local 1263, a position he held for 17 years.

Mr. Khalil's tenure as union president saw an unprecedented cooperative spirit between the Union and management that led to the successful implementation of the Faculty Personnel System, (FPS).

He worked with DLIFLC management and former 17'h District Congressman Leon Panetta on several bills to establish FPS. In 1992, Mr. Khalil along with Col. Donald C. Fischer, Jr., then the Commandant of DLIFLC, and Dr. Ray Clifford, the Provost, testified in favor of the FPS during a hearing held by the Civil Service Subcommittee of the House Post Office and Civil Service Committee. The measure was passed by both houses of Congress and signed into law in October 1992.

When the installation faced the very real possibility of closure, the Union worked tirelessly to provide statistical information to the Base Realignment and Closure Commission (BRAC) when the commission was considering moving the Institute to Fort Huachuca, Arizona in 1993 and again in 1995. In 1993, Mr. Khalil cooperated with the City of Monterey to conduct a survey of faculty asking if they would relocate out of Monterey, should the Institute move. Over half replied they • would stay in Monterey. The BRAC Commission decided not to move the Institute. When the subject came up in 1995, and again in 2005, Mr. Khalil closely cooperated with the City to make a successful case to keep DLIFLC and POM in Monterey and the Institute was spared, yet again.

Mr. Khalil's contributions to DLIFLC over his 27 year career have been significant and have served to make DLIFLC a world class language education center.

INVITATION TO ALL DLI
Alfie Khalil helped the Middle East School (then only one school) to convert all of its 150 employees to permanent status in May 1991 ❖

Alfred Galindo and Ben De La Selva at the O 'Club

Long ago and nearby -
The brief story of Alfred Galindo
DLIAA Newsletter XV - July 2007

    It was early last year (2006) when Susan Schnellbacher e-mailed the DLI Alumni Association from San Francisco stating that her nonagenarian father, Alfred Galindo, had been assigned to the Presidio of Monterey in the early 1940's. In her communiqué she explained her father was extremely eager to visit the Presidio of Monterey again, as he had not been back since his Army stint ended in the mid 40's. As security regulations mandated, Susan was told that her father, and anyone traveling with him, had to be in possession of a current and valid photo ID. Unfortunately, his last ID had expired and Susan made arrangements to secure the proper identification, in order for him to visit DLI again.

    In August 2006, Susan, her husband Charlie, brother David, son Charlie, and her 96 year old father, showed up at the Franklin Gate. As Alfred (5' 5") explained upon arrival, he had worked in the Officers Mess as Cooks Helper. His rank: Private. Thus, we immediately headed for the Officers Club. As we combed the building's first floor from front to back, Alfred would stop in every room, trying to remember what had been there. However, as there had been too many structural changes he couldn't recognize certain areas. One room he definitely recognized was his living quarters at the back of the O 'Club, on the Private Bolio Road side. As we walked, he shared many memories with us and his family.

Alfred's enlisted record revealed he was born in San Francisco, California, having been inducted into the Army on 18 July 1942 at the age of 32 years. He was discharged on 28 January 1944 and at that time had been married for two years. The "Certification for mustering out pay" was shown in his discharge papers in the amount of $200.

Alfred completed a total of one year, six months, and ten days in the military. His contributions to the military and the war effort during that time are only known to him and probably to no one else alive. However, talking with him you could sense he was a proud trooper, proud of having served his country at a time of war. We at the DLI Alumni Association and the Defense Language Institute salute Alfred for his honorable, albeit short period of service. This short article is to honor and recognize that service.

Serge Issakow (1919-2006)
Russian Teacher, Supervisor, Chair, Dean.
DLIAA Newsletter X - April 06

With input from Serge's niece, Irene Baratoff*

    Serge Issakow was born on June 26, 1919, in Ekaterinadar, Russia. Not long after his birth, his mother moved with the infant Serge to France, where he spent his early childhood. At age 13, he and his mother immigrated to Poland, where he spent his teen years.
    During WWII he moved to Austria, where he met an attractive young lady, Irene Mussin-Pushkin, his future wife. In September 1944 they were married in Vienna, where Irene gave birth to a baby girl. During that time, Serge worked as a Russian translator for the French Occupation Army in Tyrol, Austria. In July 1949, Serge immigrated to the United States with his wife and daughter and they lived in New York State until the early 1950s.
    In February 1953 Serge joined the Russian faculty of the Army Language School, becoming a Russian instructor for the ensuing 10 years. Along with another Russian instructor, Michael Chordas, Serge video-taped over 100 dialogues used in the old Russian Basic Course for many years. All students who memorized those dialogues never forgot one line in particular: "*Don't shoot, it's I, not a duck.*"
    Serge was promoted to Class Supervisor in 1963. At that time it was common for a supervisor to be in charge of 20 to 30

teachers. Peter Aikman, who came to DLI as a Russian student, and later became a teacher and supervisor, remembers that Serge was a great inspiration to students in the Foreign Area Officer (FAO) Program. Accordingly, Serge was supervisor of the FAO classes for several years. In late 1973 and early 1974 Serge became Chairperson of the Lower school. After the death of Valery Postovsky, Serge was selected Slavic Group Chief (Dean). As such, in the early 1980s he made frequent trips to the newly created Russian branch at Lackland Air Force Base, near San Antonio, Texas. - Serge retired in the spring of 1984 after 31 years of faithful service. He spoke 5 languages fluently: Russian, French, Polish, German, and English. During his journey from instructor to dean, Serge instilled the love of languages and cultures, especially Russian, to his students and teachers, and to his children and extended family. Serge moved to Rohnert Park, California in 1990 to be closer to his daughter and grandchildren.

Most of all Serge enjoyed being an instructor and supervisor because that's when he was closely involved with students. He often met with students at the Officer's Club (now the Weckerling Center), where they spoke only Russian.

Serge passed away on February 17, 2006, surrounded by his family. Of the 60 instructors that joined the Russian faculty in Feb.'53 only 3 remain living: George Bogatirev, Michael Chordas and Mr. Alexandrovsky. Irene Baratoff, his niece, who joined DLI as a Russian instructor in 1973, reports that Serge worked with her every evening for a year on how best explain to American students the complexities of Russian Grammar. That was a typical gesture of Serge, who served as a mentor and a role model to several generations of Russian teachers. Everyone who knew him misses him very much.

* Irene Baratoff was a Russian teacher and chairperson from July1973 to January 2004. She worked at both the Lackland and Monterey branches.

❖

Han Yuan "Harry" Lee (1924-2006)
Chinese Teacher, Tester, Course Developer, and Chair.
DLIAA Newsletter X - April 2006

Harry Lee was born in Tianjing (mainland) China in March 1924. He served in the Chinese Army during Second World War and immigrated to America in 1949 at the age of 25. He earned a BA degree in liberal arts at Northeastern University in Boston and in 1953, while in graduate school, was hired by the Army Language School (ALS). Harry worked with dozen other Chinese instructors who pioneered the teaching of Chinese in the early ALS/DLI years. Always trying to improve his education, in 1973 he obtained an MA in Foreign Studies from the Monterey Institute of International Studies (MIIS). After some 20 years in the classroom, Harry was trained as a Chinese Oral Proficiency Tester and worked briefly as a Faculty Trainer. In the early 1980's Harry was assigned as course writer for the Chinese Basic Course development project, later becoming its Project Officer. As such, Harry began the revision of the commercially developed Chinese course known as "Standard Chinese, a Modular Approach" or "SCAMA". A year later, Harry was asked to serve as Chinese department chairperson in the Asian School, position he occupied until his retirement in

1989. During his tenure as department chair, Harry gave impetus to the then "team teaching" program being advanced by Col. Monte Bullard, DLI Commandant. Accordingly, he established the first "teams" in the Chinese department. In the summer of 1989 Harry retired at the age of 65, after 36 years faithful federal service.

Don Damuth at POM cemetery

Grandson visits sea-going vet's grave at Presidio Cemetery –

Monterey Military News 19 May - 1 Jun 2006, p5

How many times have you driven or walked by the Presidio cemetery and wondered who was buried there? If you've passed by it at 7 a.m. and 5 p.m. you would have noticed that the American flag is faithfully raised and lowered at those times. Also, you would probably have observed that hardly anyone is ever seen inside walking around the neatly manicured lawn that grows around the tomb stones. I recently learned about someone who lays to rest there. He was a Carmel Valley resident who passed away in 1952.

The Public Affairs Office alerted me that a gentleman by the name of Don Damuth wanted to visit the graveyard where his grandfather, Wilbur Civill Damuth, had been buried. Wilbur, a veteran of the Spanish American War, WWI, and WWII, was born on Feb 25, 1875, in Atkinson, Wisconsin. Not wanting to be a farmer in Wisconsin, he lied about his age (not for the last time) and joined the Navy in September 1896 on the USS Vermont at New York, N.Y. The other time he lied was to the young lady who at the age of 16 or 17 married him. He told her he was 21, when he was really 28. She never forgave him for that.

In Feb 1897 he was given an ordinary discharge under honorable conditions as Fireman First Class. In May 1898 he reenlisted as Fireman, 2nd Class on the USS Vermont at New York, N.Y and thereafter served on the USS Restless, Vermont, Vixen, and Franklin. On 1 Dec 1898 he was discharged again on account of physical disability, under honorable conditions. In March 1917 he enrolled as a Lieutenant (JG) in the U.S. Navy Reserve, was promoted to Lieutenant, and served as Executive Officer of USS Bagley on sub-patrol outside New York Harbor. He was honorably discharged in March 1921.

When WWII broke out, Wilbur could not rejoin the Navy, as he would not have passed the physical examination required by the Navy, nor would he have been accepted due to his age, then 66. There being a shortage of engineers at that time, and desiring to serve his country, he offered his services in the Merchant Marine and was accepted. In 1942, he served as Chief Engineer on the Liberty Ship SS Ezra Meeker; ship that was carrying supplies to the forces landing in North Africa and later supplied the landings at Sicily and Salerno, Italy. One account has it that under heavy firing the Captain and First Mate were taken off the ship due to mental disturbances, and that good winds favoring them, the ship, with both a shortage of food and fuel, was brought to safety back by the Second Mate and the Chief Engineer. Wilbur returned home in such a weakened condition that he could not speak above a whisper and the sight of food, after being on concentrated food, nauseated him. He was never well after that experience.

In November 1952, upon Wilbur's death in Jamesburg, Carmel Valley, California, his wife Alpha Damuth requested a grave in the Presidio of Monterey Cemetery. Thus, Plot #376, Section D, was assigned for the burial of her husband, Lieutenant Wilbur Civill Damuth, 105-52-35, USN. At his grave site on 1 May 2006, his grandson Don stated that this "family rogue" turned out to be quite a patriot after all. ❖

Maria G. Baird (1923-2009)
Spanish Department
Teacher, Supervisor, and Chair

Read at Mrs. Baird Memorial Services in December 2009

All those who knew Maria Guadalupe Baird know that we will always remember her. Mrs. Baird was born in the state of Tamaulipas, Mexico, in 1923, of Spanish immigrant parents, who had immigrated to Mexico from Spain at the beginning of the 20th Century. By her own account she always had a love for teaching. So, she worked her way through the Mexican educational system and successfully obtained a Master's degree in Elementary and Superior Education. In her youth she taught Spanish grammar in her native Tamaulipas and then continued in the United States at Army posts where her young husband, Dewey Baird Senior, was stationed.

Around the time she became a U.S. citizen, she and her husband moved to the Monterey Peninsula. She taught Spanish at Monterey Peninsula College and in the late 50s began her long career as instructor at the Army Language School, now the Defense Language Institute or DLI. Being a very active and very knowledgeable teacher, she was promoted to class supervisor in

1966, the year when I met her. I was a soldier who had been sent to DLI to learn French, and my classes were in the same building as the other romance languages, which included Spanish.

I could observe that Mrs. Baird stood out from all the other romance language teachers in many respects. In the morning, she was the first one to arrive in the Spanish department, insuring first and foremost that every classroom had a teacher. And she moved so fast that only took her a few minutes to cross the entire hallway. I thought she was on roller skates. Any class without a teacher would get one immediately, even if she had to substitute for a sick teacher. After class hours, she would gather the twenty some teachers of her group and personally go over the grammar points and activities scheduled for the following day. A stickler for grammar, she could successfully argue the fine points of the Spanish grammar with any poor soul who dared to challenge her. And in any other discussions it was a real challenge to argue with her, for she could defend her point of view with such force as to demolish her opponent's arguments.

Because she was always teaching or visiting classes, she was very familiar with the knowledge level of the students in all the classes under her supervision. She had no mercy for unenthusiastic teachers, especially the ones who taught sitting down, did not move around the class, or who allowed students to get away with substandard pronunciation or grammar. Teachers who worked with her remember those years as some of the best of their careers. Besides learning from a master teacher, they also enjoyed the cultural hours at the International Kitchen, when Mrs. Baird personally cooked for the students, who for the first time would taste authentic Mexican food. In addition she would impart cultural lectures and would allow students to mimic their teachers' eccentricities in well-organized skits. During those years Mrs. Baird continued her professional education. When Linguistics was in vogue, she traveled to the University of California in Santa Cruz to obtain 30 units in linguistics, and knowing that DLI was paying more and more attention to education; she pursued and received a Master of Arts in 1970 from the Monterey Institute of Foreign Studies.

In the early seventies, that very active supervisor was promoted to chairperson, job she performed with the same enthusiasm and passion as her previous position of class supervisor. By then I was back at DLI, now as a Spanish instructor. Again, I saw the same professional traits I had observed several years before. In my years as a French, then Polish student I observed the habits of bad and good teachers. That experience helped me immensely working for Mrs. Baird, who in a few months promoted me to class supervisor and for which I am forever grateful. I left the Spanish department in 1976 and kept close ties with her and with the Spanish department until her reassignment to the Non Resident Division, where she worked until her retirement in 1993.

In summary, Mrs. Baird's career with DLI spanned over 35 years, years when she and many others were instrumental in transforming DLI from an excellent to an outstanding institution. She knew a lot about language education; she was a teacher's teacher, she was active and tough; She was uncompromising in her efforts to propel teachers and students towards excellence. When she retired in 1993, DLI lost one of its giants.

Mrs. Baird enlightened us to become better educators. Our Institute and our country are eternally grateful for her many years of dedication and service.

❖

HALL OF FAME
Hall of Fame Inductees - 2006
DLIAA Newsletter XII - October 2006

Mr. Leon Panetta
Mr. Leon Panetta has championed language education in the military and worked to improve DLIFLC's home at the Presidio of Monterey for more than 30 years. As a member of the U.S. House of Representatives for California's 16th/17th district from 1977 to 1993, Panetta was instrumental in providing funds for capital improvement projects on the Presidio in the late 80s and early 90s. Due to his advocacy for the Institute, Nicholson Hall, Munakata Hall, Aiso Library, Munzer Hall, Price Fitness Center and the newer troop billets have been built at the Presidio. Panetta played an essential role in the Institute being regarded as an academic institution, through his efforts to secure teacher compensation based on educational background and performance. His support in Congress of better pay for DLIFLC faculty led to the current Faculty Personnel System. Panetta has continually advocated for more and better language instruction in the United States and was a key participant in developing and gaining Congressional approval for the National Security Education Program. Linguists, diplomats, and strategists with language and cultural competencies are finally being produced by our higher education system at levels necessary to collaborate and compete on the world stage. Panetta served as chair of the House Budget Committee; Director, Office of Management and Budget; and White House Chief of Staff. He and his wife, Sylvia, founded and lead the Leon and Sylvia Panetta Institute for Public Policy.

Mr. Whitney E. Reed
Mr. Whitney E. Reed, who was commandant of the National Cryptologic School (NCS) from 1986 to 1993 and NSA/CSS Deputy Director for Education and Training, is a lifelong champion of the foreign language community, with a special concern for

military linguists. He developed a system of language training and maintenance at sites outside of DLIFLC for the Navy, and adapted it for the Air Force. Today, that system lives on as the Air Force Exportable Language Training Program, which grew exponentially with Reed's support. He also revised language training curricula to include current, authentic materials in the classroom, making classes much more relevant to military linguists. Moreover, Reed was instrumental in bringing computer technology to language teaching. He provided the first infusion of computers into both NCS and DLIFLC classrooms, and developed teaching guidelines to take advantage of their new capabilities. Perhaps most significantly, Reed impelled the Defense Language Committee to establish a realistic, measurable proficiency graduation standard of an ILR level 2 for listening, reading and speaking. To complement the new standard, he developed Final Learning Objectives for the basic course that integrate proficiency, performance, and work-focused content domains to provide the DoD with qualified and motivated linguists for the critical security challenges that face our nation. The Hall of Fame is located at Aiso Library, named for DLIFLC's first director of academic training in the 1940s.

Colonel (USAF, Retired) William P. Fife
Col. William Fife graduated from the Army Language School Russian Basic Course in 1948. He is widely considered the "Father of Airborne Intercept" for the Air Force. In a career that spanned seven decades, he helped create the Air Force Communications Intelligence (COMINT) capability. He transformed Army Security Agency equipment and organizations into the Air Force's first Radio Squadron (Mobile), created the first airborne COMINT collection program, and established Air Force Security Service (USAFSS) intercept sites at Misawa, Ashiya and Wakkanai, Japan and in Korea. Fife planned and flew on the first USAFSS COMINT recon mission in 1949, paving the way for future BLUE SKY COMINT missions. He set the standard for employment of linguists in the Air Force that continues today.

Lieutenant Colonel (USAF, Retired) Rick Francona

Lt. Col. Rick Francona graduated from DLIFLC's Vietnamese Basic Course in 1971, the Arabic Basic Course in 1974, and the Arabic Intermediate Course in 1978. He distinguished himself during numerous assignments in the Middle East, including tours as an advisor to the Royal Jordanian Air Force, liaison officer to the Iraqi armed forces during the Iran-Iraq War, and personal interpreter and advisor to General Norman Schwarzkopf during the Persian Gulf War. He was the lead interpreter for the cease-fire talks with the Iraqi Army that ended Operation Desert Storm. After the Gulf War, Francona served as the first Air Attaché at the U.S. Embassy in Syria. He also served with the National Security Agency, the Defense Intelligence Agency and the Central Intelligence Agency in the region, and developed the Defense Department's counterterrorism intelligence branch. Since retiring from the Air Force, Francona has written numerous articles and a book (Ally to Adversary – An Eyewitness Account of Iraq's Fall from Grace), and is a military analyst for NBC News.

Mr. Shigeya Kihara

Mr. Shigeya Kihara was one of the four original instructors of the Japanese language for the Fourth Army Intelligence School, the precursor of DLIFLC's, making him one of the "Founding Fathers" of the Institute. By the end of World War II, the school, then called the Military Intelligence Service Language School (MISLS), had graduated some 6,000 soldier-linguists. After the war, Kihara and his family moved with the school to the Presidio of Monterey, where he continued to teach Japanese. In 1960, he became Director of Research and Development and later, Director of Support Systems Development. He retired in 1974, after serving his country for 33 years and teaching thousands of military linguists. Upon retirement, Kihara remained active in the community. His interests in documenting the role of MISLS during World War II, and the role of Japanese-Americans during that period, led him to consult on several books, films and magazine articles documenting the contributions Japanese-American citizens made to the war effort despite being held in internment camps by the U.S. government. Kihara died on January 16, 2005.

Major General (USA, Retired) Roland Lajoie

Maj. Gen. Roland Lajoie graduated from the Army Language School Russian Basic Course in 1968. From 1973 to 1976 he served as Assistant Army Attaché to the Soviet Union, after which he commanded the U.S. Army Russian Institute in Garmisch, Germany. He later served as Deputy Director for International Negotiations, J-5, Joint Chiefs of Staff; First Director, U.S. On-Site Inspection Agency; U.S. Defense Attaché in Paris and Moscow, and Chief, U.S. Military Liaison Mission, Potsdam, East Germany. His last military assignment was as the Associate Deputy Director for Operations/Military Affairs, Central Intelligence Agency. Lajoie served in a civilian capacity as the Deputy Assistant to the Secretary of Defense for Cooperative Threat Reduction until January 1998. In December 1998 President Clinton appointed Lajoie as the U.S. Chairman to the U.S.-Russia Joint Commission on POW/MIAs, where he led efforts to uncover the fates of military personnel of both sides missing since WWII. Lajoie is a stalwart example of a military linguist using his skills in service to this country.

Major General (USAF, Retired) Doyle Larson

Maj. Gen. Doyle Larson was instrumental in the development of a career linguist force within the Air Force. He founded RC-135 COMBAT SENT Airborne Reconnaissance Units at Eielson AFB, AK, and Offutt AFB, NE. He also established the RC-135 operation at Kadena, Japan, in support of U.S. military operations in Vietnam, which is credited with saving many downed pilots, as well as numerous assists for air-to-air kills during the war. Later, Larson commanded the Electronic Security Agency (now the Air Intelligence Agency), where he developed the "COMFY OLYMPICS" language competition. This competition continues today and was the precursor to DLIFLC's Linguist of the Year competition. Larson is a fervent supporter of military crypto-linguists. Upon his retirement, he received the Order of the Sword from the Air Intelligence Agency enlisted community for his tireless dedication to bettering the lives of enlisted linguists – to include promotions, selective reenlistment bonuses, flight pay for enlisted aircrew linguists, and quality of life improvements. In retirement, Larson served as president of the Air Force Association.

Mr. Hugh McFarlane

Mr. Hugh McFarlane graduated from the Army Language School Russian Basic Course in 1966 and the Hebrew Basic Course in 1970. During nearly 23 years as a Navy linguist, he established and administered the first Naval Security Group language maintenance program, at Misawa Japan. He helped manage and then redesign the National Security Agency/Central Security Service (NSA/CSS) military linguist program, which remains the longest-lived language intern program in the cryptologic community. After retiring from the Navy in 1988, McFarlane worked for seven years at DLIFLC, where he implemented the Feedforward/Feedback information exchange system between DLIFLC and follow-on technical schools wrote a major portion of the Command Language Program manual, guided seven comprehensive curriculum reviews, and mentored more than 15,000 cryptologic students. He was the author and editor of several iterations of the cryptologic and defense training managers' Final Learning Objectives for all basic, intermediate and advanced courses, affecting over 3,000 students every year. As NSA/CSS liaison to the Office of the Secretary of Defense and the Office of the Director of National Intelligence, McFarlane has been a participant and planner in the transformation of language policy and practice in cryptology, the DoD and the Intelligence Community.

Colonel (USA, Retired) David A. McNerney

Col. David McNerney was commandant of DLIFLC from 1981 to 1985. His tenure saw a wide range of significant improvements to the Institute during a period in which the student population doubled in four years, with associated faculty expansion. He developed, articulated, and implemented a construction program for 25 new buildings at the Presidio of Monterey. These included two large General Instruction Facilities, Price Fitness Center, thirteen modern barracks buildings, nine academic and administrative support buildings, and a massive utility upgrade. He completely reorganized the Troop Command structure, replacing all leadership positions with language-specific personnel and significantly reduced the company size by activating additional companies to better support the academic program. McNerney initiated a professional development program for all assigned military linguists, which included language pro-ficiency development and the use of Military Language Instructors (MLIs). He also instituted a myriad of academic and testing initiatives, doubled the size of the permanent civilian faculty, instituted the Faculty Personnel System and created performance pay for instructors. Even more important to military linguists, McNerney developed the system of Foreign Language Proficiency Pay that was later enacted by Congress. McNerney's accomplishments in just four years had a remarkable impact on language training and linguist retention for the DoD.

Mr. Glenn Nordin
Mr. Glenn Nordin graduated from the Army Language School Russian Basic Course and the Army Russian Institute in the 1950s and the Vietnamese Advisor Course in 1966. He served as a radio interceptor with tactical forces, Operations Officer with the Army Security Agency in Berlin, a Deputy Branch Chief at NSA, a translator for the Washington-Moscow Hotline, a ground intelligence officer in Vietnam, and as Commandant of the Army Electronic Warfare School. As a defense contractor, Nordin led team development of the first all-digital workstations and on-line dictionaries for language specialists. His civil service career highlights include Executive Secretary of the Director of Central Intelligence Foreign Language Committee and as Assistant Director for Intelligence Policy (Language) with the Office of the Secretary of Defense. In these positions, he conceptualized and defended a wide variety of initiatives in foreign language education, training, processing and analysis, including a virtual language work-learning environment to facilitate workload sharing and continuing education of language specialists. His work with the Interagency Language Roundtable (ILR) brought him to national attention as an advocate for universal language education and employment. A senior DoD official dubbed Nordin the "conscience of language" in the Pentagon. He has had a tremendous impact on the day-to-day lives of linguists and greatly facilitated their work.

Hall of Fame Inductees - 2007
DLIAA Newsletter XVI - October 2007

Mr. George X. Ferguson Sr.

During WWII, then Captain George Ferguson was a critical asset to many military missions throughout his various assignments. In those years he used his language skills as a foreign contingent escort for dignitaries, chiefs of staff, cabinet ministers, and general officers visiting the United States. Additionally, his skills in both language and culture assisted with numerous military operations in Africa and Europe. Ferguson was instrumental in the then Army Language School's dramatic increase in language teaching that expanded coverage from three to twenty languages in 1947. He was appointed as Chair of the Spanish Language Department in 1948 and later advanced to the position of Chair of the Romanic Scandinavian Division, which encompassed five languages, in 1948. He, and two others, co-authored and developed an innovative total immersion approach to language learning using processes patterned after the natural instruction techniques used by parents in teaching children to speak, read, and write. This method of total sensory learning condensed the time period to create a fully proficient linguist exponentially and is still in use today.

Mrs. Ingrid M. Hirth

Ingrid Hirth served for 17 years in varying capacities at the Defense Language Institute. She was born in Czechoslovakia and fled with her family to West Germany at the end of WWII. She earned a Fulbright Scholarship and traveled to New York City where she studied French and English, which added to her previous knowledge of Czech and German. After her graduate studies in science and Latin at Frankfurt University she taught English, German, and computer programming in various countries throughout the world. She became a U.S. citizen in 1964. In 1982 Mrs. Hirth furthered her lifelong desire to teach and was hired as a German Language instructor at DLIFLC. In 1984 she served as Supervisor of the German Gateway Program for three months and earned a "Special Act Award" for development of the German Basic Course syllabus and the creation of the Air Force Exchange Scientist Course Program of Instruction. Hirth was continually lauded by her students for her enthusiasm and love of teaching and in 1985 she mentored three additional German instructors which greatly reduced student attrition rates. She earned Central European School Instructor of the

Year honors in 1992 through her classes earning an overall 96percent pass rate on the Defense Language Proficiency Test. Mrs. Hirth taught countless numbers of DOD personnel prior to her retirement as a Senior Instructor on December 31, 1998.

Colonel Thomas Sakamoto (USA, Retired)
Colonel Thomas Sakamoto was a member of the first graduating class at the Military Intelligence Service Language School at the Presidio of San Francisco. During his 28 year career as a military linguist he used his skills in many capacities. On one such assignment he provided crucial translation support to Brigadier General Thomas Chase, First Cavalry Commander. Then Technical Sergeant, Sakamoto quickly translated captured documents which provided the locations of massed Japanese troops. Chase used the information to order bombardment of the previously unknown enemy positions. Immediately following, he translated another document indicating a "Banzai" attack within 24 hours. Once again, Chase initiated bombing of the Japanese by nine Destroyers and numerous B-29 Bombers. The flawless translations of the documents saved countless lives, led to the capture of the Los Negros Islands Naval Base and earned him the first of his two Bronze Stars. Sakamoto landed ahead of General Douglas MacArthur in the occupation of Japan and provided translation during the Japanese surrender on USS Missouri. Additionally, Sakamoto served as the official translator for President Eisenhower on his trips to Okinawa and was advisor to the Director of Intelligence for the Royal Thai Army in Bangkok, Thailand. He served in various other military intelligence positions including assignments at the Sixth Army Headquarters, Headquarters U.S. Army in Vietnam and the Intelligence Headquarters Office of the Deputy Chief of Staff. Sakamoto was a Defense Language Institute student in 1949-50 when he learned Russian and again in 1964 when he returned for the Thai Basic course.

Major Masaji Gene Uratsu (USA, Retired)
Major Masaji Gene Uratsu was a member of the first graduating class at the Army Language School at Crissy Field, Presidio of San Francisco. During his career as a Japanese linguist he was assigned as a translator for numerous military operations during World War

II. On one such appointment, he was assigned to the "Bushmasters" of the 183rd Combat Regimental Team in New Guinea where he earned his first Bronze Star by persuading a group of Japanese Soldiers to surrender without incident. He earned his second Bronze Star as a member of an Interrogation of Prisoners of War team. During this posting, then a Lieutenant, Uratsu led a signal monitoring team to the war's front lines. The team was regularly bombarded during the four week endeavor. His leadership in this task ensured the completion of the critical mission with no loss of his assigned troops. Uratsu's military career culminated in his three year assignment as the Military Language Aide to the Civil Administrator of Okinawa. In that capacity he used his language skills to interpret for generals in their meetings with numerous visiting dignitaries and local newspapers. In January 1961, he assumed his final post as a staff officer of the Army Language School at the Presidio of Monterey until his retirement in April of 1962.

Mr. Benjamin De La Selva
Mr. De La Selva's linguistic career began in 1965 when he studied French at the Defense Language Institute Foreign Language Center (DLIFLC), Monterey, California. After graduating from the French course he attended the Prisoner of War (POW) interrogation course at Fort Holabird, Maryland, and in August of 1966 was assigned to the 173rd Airborne Brigade in Vietnam, where he served as a POW interrogator and French linguist. He performed those duties side-by-side with South Vietnamese soldiers, earning their respect through his knowledge of intercultural values. After one year in Vietnam Mr. De La Selva returned to DLIFLC to learn Polish and then left the Army in 1968. With a Master's Degree in Education, he was hired by DLIFLC in 1972 as a teacher and writer of the new Spanish Basic course. In the next decade Mr. De La Selva served in almost every DLIFLC directorate, including one and a half years as the Provost's Program Manager. In 1985 he became Dean to the Combined Asian and Korean school and over the following 20 years served as school dean, in charge of every major DLIFLC language program. He participated in many pioneering initiatives including Team Teaching, the Faculty Personnel System and the introduction of up-to-date teaching methods. Moreover, he led the development of

much needed Spanish, Chinese, Korean, and Arabic curricula, and for four years was head of the DLIFLC Deans' Council. During his rise from teacher to dean, he trained thousands of military linguists, guided several generations of language teachers, and mentored many supervisors and managers who now occupy leadership positions. He retired from DLIFLC in January 2005 and currently is the President of the DLI Alumni Association (http://www.dli-alumni.org), a non-profit organization he founded. On April 5, 2005, California Representative Sam Farr entered De La Selva's name and achievements into the permanent record of the U.S. House of representatives.
(http://www.thomas.gov/cgi-bin/query/R?r109:FLD001:E00543)

Hall of Fame Inductees - 2011
DLIAA Newsletter XXXII - October 2011

Major Jose Jesus Anzaldua, USMC (ret)
Marine Corps Major Jose Anzaldua was a vital asset to the conflict in Vietnam. As a Defense Language Institute West Coast (DLIWC) trained Vietnamese linguist, Anzaldua was assigned to a Combined Action Platoon on Phu Loc 6 on a small hill outside of Liberty Bridge in the Quang Nam Province of Vietnam. Then a corporal, Anzaldua was tasked with using his language skills as an Intelligence (S2) Scout for the 2nd Battalion, 5th Marine Regiment to provide security and protection for a refugee camp at the base of Phu Loc 6. On 20 January 1970, during a foot patrol, Anzaldua and a squad of scouts were captured by the Viet Cong. Anzaldua was held captive as a prisoner of war for three years. During his time as prisoner, Anzaldua was able to understand the Viet Cong's plans and communicate them to his fellow POW's. Anzaldua's language training was instrumental in his survival and that of other prisoners of war held captive by the Viet Cong.

Dr. Ray Clifford
Dr. Ray Clifford came to DLIFLC in 1981, serving first as academic dean, provost and then chancellor. He is mostly remembered for introducing the proficiency oriented instruction and for the subsequent 128 percent improvement in student results. Clifford

began his academic career in 1965 as a German language teacher in an intensive language program for missionaries. He earned a doctorate degree in foreign language education and as chancellor, supervised the largest foreign language instructional program in the United States. His greatest accomplishments at DLIFLC include: seeing the Institute through regional accreditation and subsequent degree granting authority; implementing the standardization of the Department of Defense language proficiency testing program and grading practices; helping establish a merit based faculty pay system; introducing team teaching methods as an Institute standard; and implementing the stair stepped Defense Language Aptitude Battery qualification requirements. Clifford retired from the government in 2005 but continues his career at Brigham Young University in Utah.

Dr. Martha Herzog
Dr. Martha Herzog began working for the Department of the Army in 1974 and retired after 31 years of distinguished service in 2005. During her career at DLIFLC she served in numerous academic positions including that of testing specialist, chief of non-resident instruction, and dean of three language schools. As head of the Evaluation and Standardization Directorate, Herzog was a key player in the implementation of proficiency as the organizing principle for instruction. She developed the first-ever proficiency-oriented Defense Language Proficiency Test (DLPT-III) and inaugurated the assessment of speaking proficiency at DLIFLC both in the early 1980s. As dean of Romance Languages, she collaborated with the Research Division to help prevent academic failures by sensitizing faculty and students alike to the existence and importance of learning styles and learner differences. As dean of Curriculum and Faculty Development, she continued her efforts to professionalize the faculty and lengthened the Instructor's Certification Course from two to four weeks. At Evaluation and Standardization, Herzog completed the revision of the oral proficiency testing program, leading to the deployment of the Oral Proficiency Interview 2000 with improved procedures for initial tester certification training as well as ongoing quality control.

Mr. Everette Jordan

Mr. Everette Jordan began his distinguished career as a DLIFLC language student in 1977 when he graduated from the Russian basic course and advanced Russian Le Fox program. Jordan was hired by the National Security Agency in 1983 and worked both as a Russian and Arabic linguist. In the late 90s, he took a posting as the Chairman of the Director of the Central Intelligence Foreign Language Committee where he oversaw the budget and funding of the SCOLA program. While with the DCIFLC, he led a group of Intelligence Community language technologists, translators, and instructors to work with the World Wide Web Consortium and other industry leaders to improve foreign language capabilities in databases, internet pages, and basic word processing programs. In 2002, Jordan was selected to be on the first House and Senate Intelligence Committee overseeing the issues that led to the attacks of 9/11. From 2003 to 2007, Jordan served as the founding director of the National Virtual Translation Center (NVTC) which was tasked with creating a cadre of language translators, transcribers, and interpreters nationwide, who would help with the backlog of untranslated material in the U.S. Government's possession. The NVTC now has offices stretching from Monterey to Washington D.C. to Boston and to Doha, Qatar. During this time, Mr. Jordan served as a member of the DLI Academic Advisory Board from 2004-2005 and also as a board member of the DLI Alumni Association where he is still a member at large.

Ms. Renée Meyer
Much of Renée Meyer's legacy began at the Presidio of Monterey. On assignment from the National Security Agency/Central Security Service (NSA/CSS), she developed instructional programs that reflected real-life, task-based learning for cryptologic language personnel at the Institute and in the field. She later adapted this approach from classroom to computer for language and other disciplines as Cryptologic Training Manager and NSA Associate Director for Education and Training. Meyer devoted her life to improving foreign language readiness and posture. The first NSA Senior Language Authority, she articulated operational language standards for the entire cryptologic cadre, and then created the mechanisms throughout DoD and the Intelligence Community to support their implementation for the long term. She has had a

profound impact on the ability of our country to meet its language challenges. Meyer currently lives in Maryland, where she directs a charitable company that brings beautiful ballet to people who otherwise might not have the opportunity to experience it.

Mr. Robert Tharp

Mr. Robert Tharp was by many accounts one of the most inspirational and best teachers of basic, intermediate, and advanced spoken Chinese at DLIFLC where he worked from approximately 1965 to the early 1980s. Tharp was born in China in 1913 of British missionary parents and grew up speaking Chinese. During WW II he was interned in Japan for a year. Following his release Tharp worked for British Intelligence in India fighting the Japanese until the end of WW II. After the war he went back to China and resumed his ministry and worked until 1949 when the communist forces were victorious over the nationalists and in short order began expelling missionaries from China. Upon successfully interviewing for a job with the Army Language School in the 1960s, and upon reporting for duty, Tharp surprised his colleagues who thought he was Chinese. Tharp died in 1994 but left a great legacy of several thousand students who are now found in all parts of the world.

❖

Mr. Benjamin De La Selva　　　　　Maj. DJ Skelton

DLI Alumni Association and DLI Foundation Merger
Message from the DLIAA President
DLIAA Newsletter 45 - January 2015

As most of you know, in November 2001 I founded the DLI Alumni Association (DLIAA) and have been its president since that time. In the fall of 2012, the Association sought to merge with the DLI Foundation (DLIF), and by August of the same year began transferring all its tasks and responsibilities to the latter. Thus, in the next several weeks, the "Association-Foundation" will be entirely in the able hands of the current Foundation president, Major DJ. Skelton, wounded warrior of the Iraq War, a 1998 graduate of the Chinese Basic Course; in 2008-09 he served as the Associate Dean of Middle East School I and Echo Company Commander, 229th MI Battalion. Additionally, MAJ Skelton has asked me to stay on board in an advisory capacity. For that reason, do not be surprised if in the future you see my name with titles such as "President Emeritus" or "Honorary Board Member". A letter from Mr. Skelton follows below.

Benjamin De La Selva,
DLI Alumni Association

Letter from the DLIF president.
DLIAA Newsletter 45 - January 2015

To my fellow DLI alumni:

It is my distinct honor and privilege to be able to introduce myself to you as the President/CEO of the DLI Foundation and Alumni Association. It has been a wonderful experience to work with Benjamin (Ben) De La Selva over the past few months during our transition.

I will send a separate note to all of you in the next week with my full bio and disclosing some of the many changes taking place within the Foundation and Alumni Association. I would like to take a few words to address some of the more impactful changes:

DLI Foundation and Alumni Association merger: In 2001 the DLI Alumni Association was created as a 501(c)3 non-profit organization. Ben has been building out Alumni community ever since, to include publishing a quarterly newsletter, running an annual DLI Anniversary Ball, and leading countless tours to alumni and their families. The DLI Foundation was created in 2011 as a separate 501(c)3 non-profit organization to support the DLIFLC and promote the acquisition and application of foreign language throughout the nation. As of Jan 1, 2015, these two organizations have merged into one: the Defense Language Institute Foundation. All Alumni activities will be managed as a program under the Foundation's status as a non-profit organiza-tion. If anyone has any questions concerning this merger, please feel free to contact myself, president@dli-foundation.org or our Chairman, Dino Pick at chairman@dli-foundation.org.

Website Merger: The two websites of www.dli-foundation.org and www.dli-alumni.org will be merging into one site: www.dli-foundation.org. We are currently in the process of building our new, world-class website that will facilitate providing member-only services to all of our registered alumni members. We will notify all of you as to when the new website will be launched, sometime in February, 2015. In the meantime, please feel free to write and let us know what you would like to see on our Website and what online services you would like to us to provide.

Social Media Sites: There are many social media sites (Facebook, Linkedin, Twitter, etc) that have "DLI Alumni" in the title that have been created by many alumni. It is very difficult to determine which of these sites represent the official DLI Foundation and Alumni Association. We are actively working with many owners of these sites to consolidate and "clean up" our web presence in accordance with trademark and copyright laws. We will notify you in the following weeks as to which of these sites are the official Alumni and Foundation sites. If you know of any Alumni whom have created such sites, please have them contact me. I would love to have some of these sites become our official sites.

I hope all of you and your families enjoyed this most recent holiday season! I look forward to working with and serving all of you in 2015 and the years to come. This year is a year of change and growth for the Foundation and Alumni Association. We hope you stay connected with us, tell your fellow classmates about us, and continue to help us improve on building this amazing community of graduates, faculty and staff from the number one language institute in the world, DLI!

With the utmost respect, DJ Skelton ❖

SPACE FOR YOUR NOTES

Made in the USA
San Bernardino, CA
29 May 2017